民航安检专业英语

English for Civil Aviation Security

主　编　张　宁　张　凯　黎晓霖　郝文杰

副主编　Raymond Earl Hardy

白福利　吴蔓青　吴天佑

参编者　綦　琦　李伟容　王文芳　游婷婷

胡璐施　李壮桂　李凌君　李　松

尤彧聪　王　超　臧雪梅　周雪梅

李　玉　林　聪　徐　晴　杨　静

迟皓瑜　段妩迪　宓之晴　杨嘉琪

绘图者　李依宸

清华大学出版社

北京交通大学出版社

·北京·

内 容 简 介

为了提高民航服务质量，保证民航飞机和乘客安全，进行高质量的民航安检专业英语教材编撰就显得尤为迫切。本书以民航安检的实际业务工作为出发点，按照安检业务设计学习内容，对相关业务的工作场景、工作语言进行了科学的设计和编写。本书包括口语场景对话、民航安检英语词汇学习，还专门设计了安检专业文献的阅读和翻译。本书注重知识性、基础性和应用性，力求通俗易懂，体系新颖，结构规范统一。

本书既可作为大专院校民航安检专业英语的教材，又可作为各航空公司进行安检岗位人员培训的资料，还可作为民航专业技术人员和其他从事安检工作人员的参考用书。

图书在版编目（CIP）数据

民航安检专业英语 / 张宁等主编. —北京：北京交通大学出版社：清华大学出版社，2022.2（2025.3 重印）

ISBN 978-7-5121-4648-8

Ⅰ. ① 民…　Ⅱ. ① 张…　Ⅲ. ① 民用航空–安全检查–英语　Ⅳ. ① F560.81

中国版本图书馆 CIP 数据核字（2022）第 002005 号

民航安检专业英语
MINHANG ANJIAN ZHUANYE YINGYU

责任编辑：田秀青

出版发行：清华大学出版社　　邮编：100084　　电话：010-62776969　　http://www.tup.com.cn
　　　　　北京交通大学出版社　邮编：100044　　电话：010-51686414　　http://www.bjtup.com.cn
印　刷　者：北京鑫海金澳胶印有限公司
经　　　销：全国新华书店
开　　　本：185 mm×260 mm　　印张：9　　字数：231 千字
版 印 次：2022 年 2 月第 1 版　　2025 年 3 月第 4 次印刷
印　　　数：5 001～6 000 册　　定价：35.00 元

本书如有质量问题，请向北京交通大学出版社质监组反映。对您的意见和批评，我们表示欢迎和感谢。
投诉电话：010-51686043，51686008；传真：010-62225406；E-mail：press@bjtu.edu.cn。

前　言

　　语言是人类所特有的用来表达思想、进行交流的重要工具。随着"一带一路"建设的高质量发展，现代服务业的崛起，民航产业的腾飞，民航安全的重要性日益凸显。这种世界融合的时代背景和服务产业全球化的趋势，必然对民航安检专业的人才培养提出了更高的要求。为了提高民航服务质量，保证民航和乘客安全，高质量的民航安检专业英语教材的编撰就显得尤为迫切。

　　《民航安检专业英语》是一本民航专业英语教材，旨在通过英语教学实践，夯实学生的专业语言技能，着重培养学生各种沟通能力，提高独立运用英语进行安检工作的业务素质，让学生熟悉专业英语的行文布局，掌握专业英语翻译的特点，能够阅读与自己专业相关的英语书刊和资料，使学生能以英语为工具，获取与专业相关的信息。

　　本书以民航安检的实际业务工作为出发点，按照安检业务设计学习内容，对相关业务的工作场景进行了科学的设计和编写，既有口语场景对话、民航安检英语词汇学习，还有安检专业文献的阅读和翻译的学习。本书注重知识性、基础性和应实用性相结合，力求通俗易懂，内容有新意，体系新颖，结构规范统一。学生可以通过每课的学习目标和每课后面设置的练习题，自主检测对每课内容的掌握程度。

　　本书不仅适合民航安检专业人员学习，对地铁站、高铁站、客运站，以及大型体育活动或重要会议的安检工作人员的英语学习也有很好的借鉴作用。安检从业者通过系统学习本书，有助于提升自身的文化素养和专业水平，从而更好地保证安全，提高服务水平。

　　本书由多位民航专家和语言学者共同编写。张宁、张凯、黎晓霖、郝文杰为主编，

Raymond Earl Hardy、白福利、吴蔓青、吴天佑为副主编，参编人员有綦琦、李伟容、王文芳、游婷婷、胡璐施、李壮桂、李凌君、李松、尤彧聪、王超、臧雪梅、周雪梅、李玉、林聪、徐晴、杨静、迟皓瑜、段妩迪、宓之晴、杨嘉琪，插图由李依宸绘制。

　　由于作者水平有限，书中难免有不足之处，恳请广大专家和读者批评指正。在编写本书的过程中，编者参阅了大量的书籍和文献资料，受益匪浅，在此向有关编者表示衷心的感谢！

编　者

2021 年 10 月 1 日

CONTENTS

ialogue

Passport Control

(O—security officer   P—passenger)

Dialogue 1

O: Hello, Madam.

P: Hello, I'm going to take flight CA991 to Vancouver. Is this where I pass through the security check?

O: Yes, may I have your passport and boarding pass, please?

P: Here you are.

O: Sorry, you do not have a boarding pass yet.

P: Oh, how can I get one?

O: Please go to the China Airline check-in counter, just give the airline staff your passport. They will print your boarding pass and help you check-in your luggage.

P: Thank you.

Dialogue 2

O: Hello, sir.

P: Hello. I am taking flight CA420 to Los Angeles.

O: Please show me your passport and boarding pass.

P: Here you are.

O: OK. Please wait a moment.

The security officer checks the passport and boarding pass and then returns them to the passenger.

O: OK. You can go to the gate with your carry-on baggage. Have a good trip.

P: Thanks a lot.

Dialogue 3

O: Your passport and boarding pass, please.

P: Here you are.

O: Sorry, it seems there is something wrong with your passport. Please wait here for a moment.

The security officer checks the passport and boarding pass.

O: OK. You are free to go. Please pass through the security check point along with your carry-on baggage.

P: Thanks.

Text

ACI World Outlines New Vision for Airport Security Post-Covid-19

Airports Council International (ACI) **released** its Smart Security Vision 2040, offering its vision for **seamless** airport security screening operations in the post- Covid-19 era.

The vision follows the organisation's Smart Security programme that brings together a **coalition** of airports, regulators and airlines.

ACI's vision for the future of airport security explores several long-term trends affecting aviation and airports while considering the current economic context created by the **pandemic**.

The Smart Security vision also includes **innovations** such as artificial intelligence and the increasing use of big data and stand-off detection to promote a more seamless approach to airport security screening.

These innovations have the potential to radically transform the way that passengers and baggage are screened, ACI noted.

The organisation said that it had been researching the market and seeking views from several industry experts in the field to evaluate potential advancements in aviation security screening.

ACI director general Luis Felipe said: "As the aviation industry continues to plan for a sustained recovery from **unprecedented** Covid-19 crisis, ACI believes that any **initiative** that **utilise**s improved technology to facilitate touchless and more efficient passenger journeys needs to be **accelerated**.

"The objective of Vision 2040 is to not only highlight technology and processes available today, but to look into those of the future which consider the changing needs and expectations of passengers following the Covid-19 pandemic and its effects."

Vocabulary

outline	['aʊtlaɪn]	If you outline an idea or a plan, you explain it in a general way. n. 提纲（outline 的名词复数）；要点；外形；概述 v. 画[标]出的轮廓（outline 的第三人称单数）；概述，列提纲 The methods outlined in this book are only suggestions. 本书概括的一些方法仅供参考。
Covid-19	['kɔːvid-naitiːn]	Covid-19=coronavirus disease-19；corona [kə'rəʊnə] 日冕+virus ['vaɪərəs]病毒+disease [dɪ'ziːz]疾病；2020 年 2 月 11 日，世界卫生组织正式发布通告，将新型冠状病毒感染的肺炎将正式被命名为"COVID-19"。COVID 是冠状病毒的英文词组缩写，起含义为"CO"代表 corona（冠状），"VI"代表 virus（病毒），"D"代表 disease（疾病），"19"代表疾病发现的年份 2019 年。
release	[rɪ'liːs]	If someone in authority releases something such as a

document or information, they make it available.

v. 释放；松开；发泄；解雇；（使）放松；公布

n. 释放；发行；排放；解脱

Figures released yesterday show retail sales were down in March. 昨天公布的数据显示零售额在 3 月份有所下滑。

seamless	['siːmləs]	You use seamless to describe something that has no breaks or gaps in it or which continues without stopping. *adj.* 无缝的；无停顿的；衔接完美的 It was a seamless procession of wonderful electronic music. 这是一段完美的电子音乐。
coalition	[ˌkəʊə'lɪʃn]	A coalition is a group consisting of people from different political or social groups who are co-operating to achieve a particular aim. *n.* 联合政府；（政党、社团等的）同盟，联盟 He had been opposed by a coalition of about 50 civil rights, women's and Latino organizations. 大约有 50 个民权组织、女性社团和拉丁裔社团联合起来反对他。
pandemic	[pæn'demɪk]	A pandemic is an occurrence of a disease that affects many people over a very wide area. *n.* （全国或全球性）流行病，大流行病 One pandemic of Spanish flu took nearly 22 million lives worldwide. 西班牙流感的大暴发夺去了全球近 2 200 万人的生命。
innovation	[ˌɪnə'veɪʃn]	Innovation is the introduction of new ideas, methods, or things. *n.* 改革，创新；新观念；新发明；新设施 We must promote originality and encourage innovation. 我们必须提倡创意，鼓励革新。
unprecedented	[ʌn'presɪdentɪd]	If something is unprecedented, it has never happened before. *adj.* 前所未有的，无前例的；空前的；无比的；新奇的，崭新的 Such a move is rare, but not unprecedented. 这种做法很罕见，但也不是没有先例的。

initiative	[ɪˈnɪʃətɪv]	An initiative is an important act or statement that is intended to solve a problem. *n.* 主动性；主动精神；倡议；主动权 Government initiatives to help young people have been inadequate. 政府在积极帮助年轻人方面做得还不够。
utilize	[ˈjuːtəlaɪz]	put into service; make work or employ (something) for a particular purpose or for its inherent or natural purpose *vt.* 利用，使用 Utilise group resources in the achievement of operating unit goals. 利用团体资源达成运营单位的目标。
accelerate	[əkˈseləreɪt]	If the process or rate of something accelerates or if something accelerates it, it gets faster and faster. *v.*（使）加速，加快 The government is to accelerate its privatisation programme. 政府将加快其私有化计划的进程。

译文

国际机场理事会关于新冠肺炎疫情后机场安检的新愿景

国际机场理事会（ACI）发布了 2040 年的智能安检愿景，提出了其在新冠肺炎疫情后时代机场安全检查操作的完美愿景。

该愿景遵循该组织的智能安检计划，将机场、监管机构和航空公司结为联盟。

国际机场理事会针对机场安检的愿景，考虑到疫情造成的当前经济环境，分析了影响机场安全的长期趋势。

智能安检愿景也包括了多种创新，比如人工智能和提高大数据的使用，以及远距离检测，以提高机场安检的完美程度。

国际机场理事会指出，这些创新有可能从根本上改变对乘客和行李的安检方式。

该组织表示，它们一直在研究民航市场并征求该领域多位行业专家的意见，以评估民航安全检查的潜在进步。

国际机场理事会总干事路易斯·费利佩说："ACI 认为，随着航空业筹划从史无前例的新冠肺炎疫情危机中持续复苏，任何利用革新提高非接触式安检技术和使旅客高效出行的措施，都需要加速发展。

"2040 愿景的目标不仅是强调当今可用的技术和流程，而且要展望未来，考虑新冠肺炎疫情及其影响使乘客产生的需求和期望的变化。"

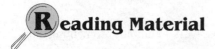
Reading Material

How to Get Through an Airport

Method 1　Before Arriving at the Airport

1

Determine whether you need to check any bags. If you use a large suitcase or more than one item of luggage, you will need to check bags. If, however, you have no more than one small suitcase and a small additional carry-on item like a backpack or purse, then you can carry on both your suitcase and your other item and avoid checking any bags.

See if you are traveling with knives, large containers of liquids, or similar items. You will not be able to carry these items onto the plane and will have to check them, regardless of the number of items you have.

2

Check into your flight and print your boarding pass. Check in online with your name and birth date or with your confirmation number that you received when purchasing the tickets. This will usually require you to specify how many bags you will be checking and choose or confirm your seating assignment. Once you've finished checking in, you will be prompted to print your boarding pass. Doing so will save you time at the airport, especially if you don't need to check bags.

3

Make sure you have all the essential documents accessible. This will include your passport or other ID, plane tickets or boarding pass, travelers' cheques, cash, travel itineraries, and any other necessary documents like a vaccination certificate, if you're going to a country where this is required. Make sure you check with your airline so that you have everything you need.

Method 2   At the Airport

1

Find out what terminal your flight will be leaving from before you arrive at the airport. Most airports have signs that clearly tell you which terminal your airline uses. At small airports, however, finding the right terminal is not something you generally have to worry about.

2

Once you arrive at the right terminal, find your check-in desk. If the airport is very large, it may have several terminals with a number of different check-in desks. There should be a list at every entrance, but if there isn't, you can ask an airport attendant. Every airline has its own travel check in desks. The name of the airline is displayed behind the counters, however the counters may not always be open when you arrive.

If you're not checking bags and have already printed your boarding pass, you can skip this step and go straight to security.

3

Talk to the check-in assistant. When you get to the counter after waiting in line, the check-in assistant will ask you some routine security questions. You need to make sure you have packed your own bags for your safety and peace of mind. The assistant will then weigh your bags to make sure they pass all weight requirements. After printing a luggage tag and giving you a baggage claim ticket to use in the case of lost bags, they will take your luggage, label it, and put it on a conveyor belt to be sent to the plane.

The check-in assistant will also ask to see your passport or ID and plane ticket or confirmation number. They will then confirm your seating assignment and print your boarding pass.

4

Make sure you know your gate number. The check-in staff usually tell you what your gate number is. If you're not sure, ask them, or find your flight on one of the many screens listing information about departing flights. Your gate number should also be on your boarding pass.

5

Go through security. All your carry-on luggage will be x-rayed and you will have to pass through a metal detector, to make sure you have nothing hidden on you which could endanger the aircraft. Airport security is there to keep both passengers and staff safe, particularly while you are in the air. Cooperate with all security procedures to help ensure everyone's safety. For instance, if you go through the scanner you may set off the alarm and this may prompt a 'pat-down' search by security staff.

For the screening, you will likely have to remove your cell phone, shoes, coat, and metallic items such as belts and pass them through the X-ray with your carry on bags. You will also have to take any laptops or small containers of liquids and gels out of your bags and pass them through the scanner in a tray provided.

6

Make your way to your gate. Find flight information such as gate and status (e.g. on time, delayed) on screens once you go through security. At your gate, there will be more detailed screens indicating when your flight has come in and when passengers will be allowed to start boarding. Also keep your ears open for any flight information which is announced over the intercom, or loud speakers. Follow signs and directions to get to your gate.

7

Wait at your gate to board. If you have time, use the restroom or grab something to eat at a nearby vendor. When your airplane is ready to board passengers it should be announced over the intercom; listen for your flight number and any other relevant information. Before you board the plane, the staff will ask to see your ID as well as your boarding pass. Keep these handy and make sure you have them ready just before you are about to board the plane.

Method 3   Leaving an Airport at the Other End More Convenient for You

1

Keep your stuff close. If you put a bag or a jacket at your feet, don't let it spill over onto the legs or feet of the person sitting next to you.

2

Get your own reading material—don't read theirs. They'll notice, and it's nosy and rude. If you're stuck in an aisle seat but still want to enjoy the view, don't lean over the person next to you to look out the window.

3

Pack headphones for any portable electronics, especially games and DVD players. Hearing someone else's music and sounds can be very irritating.

4

Don't get drunk during (or before) the flight. You may be having the time of your life, but your fellow passengers may not think so (there are airlines which don't allow any passengers on board suspected of being over the limit on alcohol consumption).

Method 4   Moving with Care

1

Be considerate of other passengers when you exit the plane. Resist the urge to push your way out first; let those nearest the exit disembark the plane first. When your turn comes, move quickly so people with connecting flights can make it in time.

2

If you know you'll need a connecting flight, think ahead and book your flight early so you can get a seat up front and exit quickly.

3

Get up to use the lavatory or to walk around only when necessary. Go through your carry-on luggage at intervals. If you need something, think ahead and retrieve items you might need later on during the flight.

4

When you get up, don't yank on the seat in front of you for support; use the seat armrests. If you want to get up but there is one or more passengers between you and the aisle, politely request that they get up to let you pass. Don't try to clamber over them; apart from the discomfort this will inevitably cause, you might injure yourself/them if you lose your balance and fall.

Tips

Clean up after yourself. Don't leave your trash stuffed in the seat pocket, blankets and pillows thrown about, crackers littered all over the seat and floor, etc. An airplane seat should be left as close as possible to how it was found. This will make "flipping the airplane" much faster for the maintenance crew and keep flights on time.

If you plan on taking a sleeping pill, opt for a window seat so passengers aren't required to climb over you in order to access the restroom.

At security, the fewer "things" you are carrying, the better. Leave all your jewelry, keys, spare change, iPod, phone, newspaper etc, in your bag. If you think your belt might set off the metal detector, take it off before security, put it in your bag, so you can put it back on afterward.

Remember that babies and children don't understand airplanes and pressure differences in their ears. Even the best behaved baby will cry during the takeoff and descent portion of the flight. Feeding a baby or giving him a pacifier can help; the sucking motion can help equalize pressure.

When movies start, ask the passenger next to you if they'd prefer to have the window shade down. The sun's rays can create an annoying glare on the television monitor, making it harder to see a view from a specific seat in the airplane. The person next to you may or may not be bothered by this; sometimes they'd prefer to have the light from the window.

Make sure you are aware of the new security rules (amount of allowable liquids in a small plastic ziplock bag etc). Security checks are delayed every time somebody tries to get through with items which are not allowed.

Keep your conversations to a low whisper if you're traveling with someone. If you speak too loudly, you'll interrupt someone's sleep or annoy your fellow passengers.

If you have a habit of removing your shoes because you're flying a long distance, make sure you don't have foot odor.

At the baggage claim, stand back from the carousel until you see your bag approaching, then step forward to retrieve it.

Do not put your feet up on the bulkhead if you are sitting by it. It's ill-mannered. If you must raise your feet, put your bag on the floor and put your feet on that.

Warnings

Remember that even if you wear headphones while you listen to loud music, your direct neighbor can hear it, and will likely be less than pleased about it. Turn your music player to a more moderate level for the flight.

Do not pack strong smelling foods (e.g. tuna sandwiches, anything with onions, deli, etc.) to eat on the plane. Your fellow passengers may be sensitive to the smell.

Exercises

1. Vocabulary

(1) One (　　) of Spanish flu took nearly 22 million lives worldwide.

    A. plague   B. fever   C. illness   D. pandemic

(2) Figures (　　) yesterday show retail sales were down in March.

    A. held   B. insisted   C. illness   D. released

(3) The government is to (　　) its privatisation programme.

    A. increase   B. accelerate   C. heighten   D. enhance

(4) We must promote originality and encourage (　　).

    A. innovation   B. create   C. invention   D. development

(5) It was a (　　) procession of wonderful electronic music.

    A. halt   B. careless   C. ceaseless   D. seamless

2. Dialogue

(1) P: Hello, I'm going to take flight CA991 to Vancouver. Is this where I pass through the security check?

    O: Yes,（我可以检查您的护照和登机牌吗？）

    P:（给你。）

(2) O: Your passport and boarding pass, please.

    P: Here you are.

    O:（对不起，您的护照有点问题，请等一下。）

3. Translate

(1) It now takes just over ten minutes to complete all the necessary procedures and travel from the airport entrance to the boarding gate.

(2) Just last week, we were required to have our electronic boarding passes or ID cards scanned before boarding, but now we can directly board the plane thanks to Facial Recognition (FR) technology.

(3) Once you have received the boarding pass when you check-in through mobile app/online/ self service kiosk, you can check-in your baggage using that.

(4) Once the verification is done, you can view your flight details in the screen.

(5) Airplane, fixed-wing aircraft that is heavier than air, propelled by a screw propeller or a high-velocity jet, and supported by the dynamic reaction of the air against its wings.

 ialogue

Going Through the Security Gate

Dialogue 1

O: Excuse me, sir. Please put all your bags on the belt to be checked.

P: OK.

O: Take off your shoes, take the personal items out of your pockets, and place it all into the trays, please.

P: Everything?

O: Oh, things like keys, coins, cell phone, cigarettes, your wallet and so on.

P: And should I take off my watch as well?

O: Yes, of course.

P: Now, is it OK?

O: Yes. Now please go through the X-ray machine.

The passenger goes through the X-ray and no alarm goes off.

O: Please take all of your things with you. Have a safe trip.

P: Thanks a lot.

Dialogue 2

O: Excuse me, sir, please put your carry-on baggage on the belt.

P: OK.

O: You need to remove any electronic devices from your bags as well as any liquids.

P: I have a laptop, an iPad and a phone charger.

O: You will need to take all of them out of your bag, and place them in a separate tray.

The passenger goes through the X-ray, no alarm goes off.

O: Please collect all of your belongings. There is a table over there where you can take your things back and put them into your baggage.

P: Thank you.

Dialogue 3

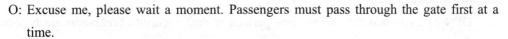

Two passengers want to go through the gate together.

O: Excuse me, please wait a moment. Passengers must pass through the gate first at a time.

One passenger decides to go through the gate first.

O: Please put all your baggage on the belt and take all the personal items out of your pockets and put them in the tray.

P: I'm sorry. There is some contact lens cleaner in my baggage.

O: Oh, please remove all liquids from your baggage to be checked.

P: OK.

Passenger goes through the X-ray and no alarm goes off.

O: Yes, you are all set. Please take all of your belongings with you. Have a good trip.

P: Thank you.

O: Next, please.

ext

How Denver International Airport's Security Screenings Are Changing

If you had to fly during the pandemic, the silver lining of having a half-full airport to breeze through probably won't last much longer. Denver International Airport officials predict summer travel in Colorado will likely hit 2019 levels as coronavirus restrictions continue to loosen.

Daily traveler counts across the nation show that movement over the past several days is more than triple what it was last year. DEN officials said that number, called "**throughput**," will only increase.

"Travel volumes at DEN have rapidly increased over the past several months and we anticipate this trend will continue throughout the summer," said Colorado Transportation Security Administration director Larry Nau.

DEN officials said the busiest time periods at their security checkpoints are between 5 a.m. and 11 a.m., noon and 2:00 p.m., and 9:00 p.m. and midnight. Those peaks are driven by an increasing number of flights departing from DEN, which has caused the return of long wait times at checkpoints.

Hopefully, a faster TSA security checkpoint

After facing a slow year, the TSA is working to fill gaps in their staffing and workflow to prepare for the oncoming **horde** of summer travelers.

A major change will be how bag screenings work. By using computed **tomography** technology, much like what hospitals use, passengers won't have to take electronics and food out of their carry-on baggage.

"This additional capability is really helpful to our officers because by getting that better view of the contents of the carry-on bag, it reduces the number of bag checks," said TSA spokeswoman Lorie Dankers. "We're coming out of a pandemic. But as a traveler, you don't want people to touch your bag or officers don't want to open your bag."

This doesn't mean the TSA's prohibited items list has changed. Weapons, firearms and **flammables** are still not allowed. And don't even think about bringing that large jar of peanut butter. It will only end in heartbreak.

Passengers also do not have to provide a boarding pass to TSA agents. Instead, they'll place their photo ID in a scanner, which will show **biographical** and flight information to the agent.

Both of these new technologies have been rolled out over the last few months at various airports across the country. Lorie Dankers said they help reduce potential touch points between passengers and security officers.

COVID-19 protocols still in place

Aside from the uptick in activity at DEN, COVID-19 restrictions are still largely in place.

The federal requirement to wear a mask at airports, even for the fully **vaccinated**, has been extended until September 13. Failure to comply could result in being denied entry to the airport or airplane, or civil **penalties**.

Security officers will also be required to wear masks and gloves at screening checkpoints. Shared and commonly touched surfaces, like screening bins, will be regularly **disinfected**.

The Centers for Disease Control requires travelers going outside the United States to provide proof of a **negative** COVID-19 test result before boarding a flight to return home, regardless of vaccination status.

Vocabulary

throughput	['θru:pʊt]	The throughput of an organization or system is the amount of things it can do or deal with in a particular period of time. n. 生产量，生产能力，吞吐量；流率 There's still a reasonable throughput of business. 业务量仍然可以。
horde	[hɔːd]	If you describe a crowd of people as a horde, you mean that the crowd is very large and excited and, often, rather frightening or unpleasant. n. 一大群；游牧部落 A horde of children ran over the office building. 一大群孩子在办公大楼里到处奔跑。
tomography	[təˈmɒɡrəfi]	(medicine) obtaining pictures of the interior of the body n. X 线断层摄影术

The CT — short for computerized tomography scan — can detect injuries and tumors.　CT 扫描（电脑断层扫描）可以检测损伤和肿瘤。

flammable　['flæməbl]　Flammable chemicals, gases, cloth, or other things catch fire and burn easily.

adj. 易燃的，可燃的

Clean up spilled medicines, bleaches and gasoline and other flammable liquids.　清除溢出的药品，漂白剂、汽油和其他易燃易爆液体。

biographical　[ˌbaɪə'græfɪkl]　Biographical facts, notes, or details are concerned with the events in someone's life.

adj. 传记的；关于生平的

History is a facsimile of events held together by finally biographical information.　历史，就是一部举行最后一起事件的履历资料传真。

protocol　['prəʊtəkɒl]　A protocol is a plan for a course of medical treatment, or a plan for a scientific experiment.

n. 礼仪；（外交条约的）草案；（数据传递的）协议；科学实验报告（或计划）

What is your lab's protocol for the collection of any monetary evidence?　你们实验室对于货币证物收集有何规程？

vaccinate　['væksɪneɪt]　If a person or animal is vaccinated, they are given a vaccine, usually by injection, to prevent them from getting a disease.

vt. 给……接种疫苗

vi. 注射疫苗，接种疫苗

What else do we need to do besides vaccinate?　除了提供疫苗之外，我们还需要做什么？

penalties　['penəltiz]　Penalty is a punishment that someone is given for doing something which is against a law or rule.

n. 惩罚（penalty 的名词复数）；刑罚；害处；足球点球

Nearly 5,000 people a year are put behind bars over motoring penalties.　每年有近 5 000 人因违法驾车

		而入狱。
disinfected	[dɪsɪn'fektɪd]	If you disinfect something, you clean it using a substance that kills germs.
		v. 除去（感染），给……消毒（disinfect 的过去式和过去分词）
		Is the Public Area disinfected upon the fixed time? 酒店的公共区域是否定时消毒?
negative	['negətiv]	If a medical test or scientific test is negative, it shows no evidence of the medical condition or substance that you are looking for.
		adj. 消极的；否定的；负的；阴极的
		v. 拒绝；否定
		n. 底片；（化验或科学实验中的）阴性结果；坏的事情
		So far 57 test-takers have taken the test and all have been negative. 到目前为止，参加测试的有 57 人，测试结果均为阴性。

译文

丹佛国际机场安检的变化

如果你不得不在新冠肺炎疫情期间乘坐飞机，那么航班只有一半客满的情况可能不会持续太久。据丹佛国际机场的官员预测，随着对新冠肺炎疫情管控的继续放松，科罗拉多州的夏季旅游出行人数可能会达到 2019 年的水平。

全国每日旅客人数显示，过去几天的旅客人数是去年同期的三倍多。丹佛国际机场的官员表示，这个被称为"吞吐量"的数字只会增加。

"过去几个月丹佛国际机场的旅客数量迅速增加，我们预计这一趋势将持续整个夏天。"科罗拉多州运输安全管理局局长拉里·诺说。

丹佛国际机场的官员说，他们的安全检查站最繁忙的时间段是：上午 5 点到 11 点，中午和下午 2 点，以及晚上 9 点和午夜。这些高峰时段是越来越多的航班从丹佛国际机场出发造成的，这导致旅客在检查点等待时间过长。

希望有一个更快的安全检查站

经历了漫长的一年之后，美国运输安全管理局（TSA）正在努力改进其人员配备和工作流程方面的不足，为即将到来的夏季旅行旺季做好准备。

一个主要的变化将是行李检查的方式。通过使用像医院一样的计算机断层扫描技术，乘客就不必从随身行李中取出电子产品和食物。

"这种额外的功能对我们的安检员真的很有帮助，因为可以更清楚地查看随身行李中的物品，减少了行李检查的次数，"美国运输安全管理局女发言人洛里·丹克斯说，"我们正在摆脱疫情。但作为一名旅客，你不希望有人碰你的行李，或者工作人员也不想搜你的包。"

这并不意味着美国运输安全管理局的违禁物品清单已更改。武器、火器和易燃物仍然不允许携带。甚至如果想携带大罐花生酱，只会以失望告终。

乘客也不必向美国运输安全管理局的工作人员提供登机牌。相反，他们会将带有照片的身份证件放在扫描仪中，扫描仪会给工作人员显示个人信息和航班信息。

过去几个月，各个机场已经推出了这两项新技术。洛里·丹克斯表示，它们有助于减少乘客和安检人员之间的潜在接触点。

新冠肺炎疫情协议仍然有效

除丹佛国际机场的活动增加以外，新冠肺炎疫情的许多限制措施仍在实施。

联邦政府要求旅客在机场戴口罩，即使是已接种全部疫苗的人也要戴口罩，这项规定已延长至 9 月 13 日。不遵守规定可能会导致被拒绝进入机场或登机，或受到民事处罚。

安检人员也将被要求在安检处佩戴口罩和手套。共用和经常接触的表面，如安检筐，将定期消毒。

美国疾病控制中心要求出国的旅客在境外登机回国之前，不论是否接种疫苗都要提供一份新型冠状病毒测试结果为阴性的证明。

Reading Material

How to Go Through Airport Security Smoothly

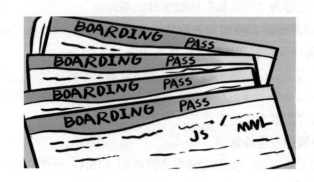

As a result of numerous hijackings, including the infamous 9/11 hijackings, airport security has heightened drastically. It leaves most travelers dreading the once enjoyable airport experience. Long lines, intrusive officers, and grumpy flyers make the Airport Security Checkpoint a less than desirable aspect of air travel. By following these steps, you will "soar" through this portion of your journey with ease.

1

Pack light and follow any rules your airport has on sizes, quantity, and restrictions. First, pack only what you need to survive; second, what you need to do first; and third, what you need to do last. If you question anything you're packing, then don't pack it. You'd be better safe than sorry. Remember that you can most likely buy it from where you're going. If not, and you don't need it to survive, then don't worry about it.

2

Be prepared. Before you get to the airport, take the necessary precautions to make your experience as simple as possible.

Wear practical shoes. Slip-on shoes will be easier to remove quickly. Of course, make sure they are comfortable enough for standing in long security lines. If you're under 13, you can wear any types of shoes, as long as they don't set off the metal detector. Also, if your 75 or in precheck you don't have to remove shoes either.

Avoid metallic clothing or accessories, as you will have to remove these before going through a metal detector. The same applies to metal items in your pockets.

Package liquids and gels appropriately. All liquids in your carry-on bag must be in bottles of three ounces or less, and all these bottles must then be placed in a clear, quart-size, zip-style plastic bag. There are a few exceptions to this rule, including milk for infants and liquid medications, but be sure to check before you pack anything. If your in pre-check you can keep your 3-1-1's items in your carry on.

Pack your belongings in an organized way, so that if there is a problem, they can open your bag, check things out, and move on.

Avoid contraband. Check beforehand to make sure that anything you will bring along, whether in your checked luggage or your carry-on, is allowed on the plane. Otherwise, you may be forced to throw these items away or even face questioning and/or prosecution.

3

Have your boarding pass and Photo ID (driver's license or passport) in your hand prior to getting in the security line. The line, although long at times, can move quickly, and seasoned travelers can get irritated with anyone that holds up the line digging for the necessary papers.

4

Pay close attention to directions while you wait in line. It pays to see what other passengers forget.

5

Put your boarding pass and ID away as soon as they've been checked. Keep your boarding pass in your pocket, as it will be screened again, but put your ID back into your bag to keep it secure.

6

Remove the necessary items from your carry-on as soon as you get to the belt. Place these items, along with your carry-on, directly on the belt or in the provided bins. Most airports require that you remove any plastic bags full of liquids and any laptops from your carry-on bag, but be sure to follow instructions. If you have completed a "TSA PRE CHECK", then don't remove your 311s from your bag or your laptop from its case.

7

Make removing your shoes easy. The TSA requires passengers to remove their shoes when passing through the metal detector. There is not much room to squat down. People will try to pass around you, and benches are inconveniently far from your bags. Wear shoes that you can slip off without bending down or undo your laces before getting in line and tuck them into your shoe. This way, you will be able to slip them off easily to be placed on the X-ray belt. If you're under 13, keep your shoes on while walking through the metal detector, unless they have metal on them. Also, if you're over 75, you can keep your shoes on. Keep your shoes on if you have completed a TSA PRE CHECK.

8

Remove all necessary clothing and accessories from your body. Take off any metal objects, as well as jackets and hats, depending on the airport. If you're under 13, over 75, or in TSA PRE CHECK, leave your jackets on unless if they have metal. Kids under 13 can leave their hats on.

9

Stay calm before your flight. Don't think about work, bills, or anything that could stress you out. Think about the adventure you're about to have or just had, and how long you're going to remember it for.

10

Don't be afraid of the security guards. Be polite and respectful, and do as you're told. Remember, if you don't have anything illegal on you, you're good. The security guards are there for your safety, not to scare you. If you don't have TSA PRE CHECK or anything that is "faster" than a regular line, you will have to take your shoes off and wait a little longer. This is nothing to stress about; it just adds to the safety of your flight.

11

Step through the metal detector when an employee of the airport waves you through. If you are selected for additional screening, comply immediately and politely. Tell security if you have any piercings or surgical implants, or any metal in or on your body that you can't remove. Remember to take off all jewelry that is metallic and lay it in the component bins that will be traveling into the X-ray machine.

12

Try not to be noticeably stressed out. This makes you look suspicious like you have something to hide. In your head, tell yourself "I have nothing to hide" repeatedly.

13

Tell the security guards that security checks make you nervous. It's okay to be nervous for a serious TSA check. They will most likely try to help you in any way you need or reassure you. They are people too, and you aren't the first person to be stressed by security.

14

Collect your belongings and put them away. Making sure you have everything you need. Leave the security area quickly, making way for other passengers.

Tips

Check with international regulations to see what is permitted to fly. In most scenarios, toxic chemicals, liquids not following the 100 ml/L rule, weapons, lithium batteries, recalled electronics, and certain household items will not be permitted onboard the airplane to prevent accidents.

Remaining calm and avoiding suspicious or anxious behavior will go a long way, especially if you are pulled aside for additional searches.

If you are asked to step aside for additional search be courteous and respectful. The security people are only doing their job.

Try not to have a lot of change in your pockets. You will have to drop all of it into the bins. Picking up a bunch of change, coupled with putting on shoes and rounding up your possessions, can be tedious.

Place small items such as loose change, watch, mobile phone or keys into your coat pocket or carry on luggage while in line. You can sort out your items at your leisure in the departure lounge.

Put all your loose change in a purse or wallet. Put all the things that are likely to cause you to get searched at the top of your bag so you can take them out quickly and easily.

If you're under the age of 13, you generally will not have to remove your shoes during the security screening. You may also get multiple passes through the metal detector or advanced technology, and you are likely to have your hands swabbed.

If you are traveling internationally, you will need to keep your passport with you. You will need it upon check-in, primary security screening, any passport control stations between you and your gate, any additional screenings, and at the gate. You will also need it when you deplane.

Know that everyday items (such as batteries) can pose a severe hazard to passengers on board an airplane.

While waiting in line, take this time to prepare for getting through the security metal detector/X-ray conveyor belt. Remove any laptops from bags, remove your footwear, etc. When you get to the "buckets", all you need to do is drop your items and slide them onto the conveyor belt. If you are traveling with another person, have them assist you with holding things and vice versa.

If you are part of the TSA approved traveler program, then you can keep your shoes on along your belt and your jacket. You also keep your 3-1-1's items in your bag and your laptop in its case. You also take kids under 13 with you through the pre-check.

Warnings

Don't make any jokes, especially those that relate to bombs or terrorists, when going through security. Airlines are required to take possible threats seriously, and you could get into huge trouble.

Keep your boarding pass and passport handy. Do not put them in the checked in luggage, as this will cause a lot of problems.

Listen to any security screener instructions and do as they say. Remember that all this security is to help keep you safe.

Be prepared for searches on certain kinds of connecting flights, such as if you are flying standby and must get off, claim baggage and check in at a gate to get onto the next leg of your trip!

Exercises

1. Vocabulary

(1) Clean up spilled medicines, bleaches and gasoline and other (   ) liquids.

A. corrosive   B. flammable   C. explosive   D. radioactive

(2) Is the Public Area (   ) upon the fixed time?

A. infected   B. disinfected   C. checked   D. inspected

(3) What else do we need to do besides (   )?

A. vacation   B. vaccines   C. vaccinate   D. immune

(4) So far 57 have taken the test and all have been (   ).

A. negative   B. acidic   C. alkalinity   D. recessive

(5) There's still a reasonable (   ) of business.

A. go through   B. through   C. throughout   D. throughput

2. Dialogue

(1) O: Excuse me, sir.（请把您的包放在传送带上）.

P: OK.

O:（请脱鞋，拿出口袋中的随身物品），and place it all into the trays, please.

(2) O:（哦，诸如钥匙，硬币，手机，香烟，钱包等。）

P:（我的表也要摘下来吗?）

O: Yes, of course.

3. Translate

(1) An airplane's essential components are the body or fuselage, a flight-sustaining wing system, stabilizing tail surfaces, altitude-control devices such as rudders, a thrust-providing power source, and a landing support system.

(2) Most airplanes are designed to operate from land; seaplanes are adapted to touch down on water, and carrier-based planes are modified for high-speed short takeoff and landing.

(3) Dubai's aviation sector has been at the forefront of a global campaign to restore vital international air services with the opening of quarantine-free travel corridors between the UAE and multiple countries around the world.

(4) We have preliminarily gained new ground in airport security, operations, and services.

(5) We actively use new technologies, such as big data and AI to innovate new smart airport construction modes.

Lesson **Three**

Dialogue

Checking with Hand Detector

Dialogue 1

When the passenger went through the security gate, the alarm setoff.

O: Excuse me, do you still have any metal items on you?

P: No. My pockets are empty.

O: Good. Please stand on the platform.

P: OK.

Checks the passenger with the hand detector and they can hear the beeping sound.

O: There is some metal in your pocket.

P: I'm sorry. I forget that I have some coins in my hip pocket.

O: Please take them out.

Checks the passenger with the hand detector and there is no beeping sound.

O: That's all. You can leave now.

P: Yes.

O: Don't forget your belongings. Have a good journey.

P: Thank you.

Dialogue 2

O: Please take off your shoes and step over here. Stand on the platform, please. Your shoes should be X-rayed separately.

P: But, is the floor clean?

O: Don't worry. The mat has been disinfected. Now hold out your arms and stand with your feet apart, please.

The officer uses the hand detector to check the passenger.

O: You are all set.

P: May I go now?

O: Of course, please do not forget any of your belongings.

P: Thank you.

Dialogue 3

O: This way please. Hold out your arms and stand with your feet apart on that platform.

P: Excuse me, I'm afraid I cannot be checked by X-ray.

O: Why not?

P: I have a pacemaker. I have a card from my doctor explaining the risk of an X-ray.

O: Oh, I see. Then we will check you by hand.

P: Yes, that will be necessary.

The officer checks the passenger manually.

P: May I go now?

O: Yes, you are all set.

P: Thank you.

O: Have a good trip.

Text

Airport Security Carry-On Regulations

What You Can and Cannot Put In Your Carry-On Luggage

The United States Transportation Security Administration (TSA) has established a set of rules for airline passengers at security checkpoints in airports about what they can and cannot bring with them as they fly.

New security check-in policies are periodically updated, including the items allowed and prohibited aboard aircraft.

General Rules

The TSA has rules for eight categories of items you can bring with you as you fly, whether in the passenger cabin with you as carry-on luggage or in the cargo hold as checked bags. This list includes the rules that apply in every situation, as well as banned specific items as of February 4, 2018.

The number of carry-on items you can bring is established by the individual airline: most say you can bring one carry on, and one personal item. Pack your carry on in neat layers and place your liquids bag on the top.

Hazardous materials (HAZMAT) are not allowed on planes at all. **Prohibited** items include cooking fuels, explosives, and according to FAA regulations, some high-alcohol content beverages.

The 3-1-1 Rule

Liquids, gels, creams, pastes, and **aerosols** are only allowed as carry-on items according to the 3-1-1 Rule. No container may be larger than 3.4 ounces (100 ml). The travel containers must all fit in a single one-quart-sized bag and kept in your carry-on, to **facilitate** the screening process.

Exceptions to the 3-1-1 rule include medically-necessary liquids, medicines, and creams: you can bring larger quantities, and you don't need to put your medications in a plastic bag.

However, any liquid, aerosol, gel, cream or paste that sets off alarms during screening will require additional screening.

Flammables

Flammables are anything that can be easily set on fire. As you might imagine, many of those are banned completely from airplanes, but there are exceptions.

- Acceptable Flammable Carry-Ons: cigarettes and cigars and safety matches, disposable and Zippo lighters, phone chargers, power banks, dry batteries, solid (but not gel) candles.
- Checked Luggage Only: rainbow flame crystals, gel candles, and self-defense sprays.
- Completely Banned: Any flammable liquid fuel, such as cooking fuel, **butane**, **chlorine** for pools, bang snaps, blasting caps, and firecrackers.

Rules for **lithium** batteries have significantly changed recently. Batteries with 100-watt hours or less may be carried in a device in either carry-on or checked bags. Loose lithium batteries are prohibited in checked bags.

Firearms

In general, the TSA does not allow firearms or indeed anything that looks like or could be used as a weapon to be carried on. Firearms including ammunition, BB guns, compressed air guns, flare guns, and gun parts, may be carried in checked baggage if you meet the guidelines for transporting firearms. Essentially, the firearms must be unloaded and placed in a locked hard-sided container, which must completely secure the firearm. When you check your bag, be sure to tell the airline agent that you are checking firearms.

- Acceptable Fire Arm Carry-ons: Holsters, rifle scopes, empty shell casings.
- Checked Luggage Only: Ammunition, BB and compressed air guns, firearms, flare guns, gun parts, pellet guns, realistic replicas, rifles, shell casings, starter pistols.
- Completely Banned: flares, gun lighters, gunpowder.

Food

Liquid foods must meet the liquid standards to be carried on board, but in most cases, they can be brought in checked baggage.

Meat, seafood, vegetable and other non-liquid food items are permitted in both carry-on and checked bags. If the food is packed with ice or ice packs in a cooler or another container, ice or ice packs must be completely frozen when brought through screening. You can pack frozen perishables in your carry-on or checked bags with dry ice. The FAA limits you to five pounds of dry ice that is properly packaged (the package is vented) and marked.

Frozen liquid items are allowed through the checkpoint as long as they are frozen solid when presented for screening. If frozen liquid items are partially melted, slushy, or have any liquid at the bottom of the container, they must meet 3-1-1 liquids requirements.

Water, formula, breast milk and baby food for babies are allowed in reasonable quantities in carry-on bags; see the special instructions for travel with children.

- Acceptable Food Carry-ons: solid foods such as bread, candy, cereal, coffee beans; fresh fruit, meat, and vegetables; eggs, frozen foods if solid-frozen, baby formulas, and food.
- Checked Luggage Only: Liquids and creamy foods like honey, gravy, peanut butter, and creamy dips if they don't meet the 3-1-1 rules.
- Completely Banned: alcoholic beverages over 70% alcohol (140 proof).

Household and Tools

Household items, in general, may be brought aboard unless they have blades or could otherwise be used as a weapon (axes and blenders, cattle prods, crowbars, cooking spray, cast iron skillets). Most of those may be placed in checked baggage.

Items such as butane curling irons may be carried on board but not in the cargo hold. Power tools and regular tools larger than 7 inches are prohibited from carry-on. Liquid items (detergents and deodorants, hand sanitizers) must follow the liquid 3-1-1 rules.

Most laptops and cell phones can be brought on board or in checked luggage. The Samsung Galaxy Note 7 is permanently banned from airline travel.

- Acceptable Household Carry-ons (examples): cell phones, blenders, corded curling irons, coffee makers, detergents, computers, fidget spinners, game consoles, laptops, light bulbs, paintings, remote control cars, radios, sewing machines, staplers, tattoo guns.
- Checked Luggage Only: axes and hatchets, drills and drill bits, hammers, heating pads, mallets, Magic 8 ball, nail guns, power tools and tools larger than 7 inches.
- Banned from Checked Luggage: butane curling irons.
- Completely Banned: alcoholic beverages over 70% alcohol (140 proof), cooking spray, engine powered equipment with residual fuel, Samsung Galaxy Note 7, spillable batteries, spray starch, turpentine and paint thinner.

Medical

The TSA allows exceptions to the 3-1-1 rule for medically necessary liquids, gels, and aerosols. You can bring in reasonable quantities for your trip, but you must declare them to TSA officers at the checkpoint for inspection. It is recommended, but not required, that your medications be labeled to facilitate the security process: check with state laws about appropriate labeling. Used syringes are allowed when transported in a Sharps disposal unit or another similarly hard-surfaced container.

Personal medical oxygen cylinders are permitted if the regulator valve has not been tampered with or removed. Allowed carryons that require additional screening: nebulizers, CPAPs, BiPAPs, APAPs, unused syringes. If you have bone growth stimulator, spinal stimulator, neurostimulator, port, feeding tube, insulin pump, ostomy bag, or other medical device attached to your body, you may require additional screening. Consult with the manufacturer of the device to determine whether it can safely pass through the X-ray, metal detector or advanced imaging technology for screening.

See the TSA's Disabilities and Medical Conditions for more information.

- Acceptable Medical Carry-ons: blood sugar test, canes, casts, contact lens solutions, contacts, crutches, EpiPens, external medical devices with special, eye drops, inhalers, insulin, insulin pumps and supplies, life vests, liquid vitamins, liquid medications, pills, nitroglycerine pills, pill cutter, prosthetics, supplements, support braces, thermometer, unused syringes, vitamins, walkers, and wheelchairs.

- Completely banned: Medical marijuana is prohibited in carry-on or checked baggage.

Sharp Objects

In general, you are prohibited from traveling with sharp objects in your carry-on bags; but all can be packed in your checked bags. Sharp objects in checked luggage should be sheathed or securely wrapped to prevent injury to baggage handlers and inspectors.

- Acceptable Sharp Carry-ons: cigar cutters, crochet hooks, disposable razor, knitting needles, nail clippers, pencil sharpeners, safety pin, scissors (if less than 4 inches from the pivot point）, sewing needles, tweezers.

- Checked Baggage Only: corkscrews, box cutters, ice picks and axes, knives, leatherman tools, meat cleavers, pocket knives, razor, sabers, safety razor with blades, saws, swiss army knives, swords, throwing stars.

Sporting & Camping

Sporting and camping equipment are generally acceptable as carry-ons, with the exceptions of things that are classed as hazardous materials (such as some aerosol insecticides), things that could be used as weapons, liquids that don't follow the 3-1-1 rules and objects that are too large for the specific airline's guidelines.

Camp stoves are allowed in carry-on or checked bags only if they are empty of all fuel and cleaned so that no fuel **vapors** or residue remain. Please wrap cords and layer items in bags so officers can get a clear view of the items. You may bring a life vest with up to two oxygen cartridges inside, plus two spare cartridges in your carry-on or checked bag.

Sharp fishing tackle that may be considered dangerous, such as large fish hooks, should be sheathed, securely wrapped, and packed in your checked bags. Like other high-value objects, you may wish to pack expensive reels or fragile tackle that does not pose a security threat in your carry-on bags.

- Acceptable Sporting Carry-ons: baseballs, basketballs, footballs, bocce balls, bowling balls, bicycle chains and pumps, boxing gloves, empty coolers, divot tools, football helmets, golf balls, golf tees, hand warmers, helmets, longboards, navigation GPS, nerf guns, rocks, sand, skates, sleeping bag, small fishing lures, snowboards, snowshoes, sports cleats, tennis rackets, trophy, vacuum sealed bags.
- Checked Baggage Only: baseball bats, bowling pins, bows and arrows, canoe/kayak paddles, cast iron cookware, crampons, cricket bats, golf clubs, hiking poles, hockey sticks, kubatons, lacrosse sticks, martial arts weapons, nunchucks, pool cues, shoe and snow spikes, ski poles, snow cleats, spear guns, tent spikes, walking sticks.
- Completely Banned: bear bangers, small compressed cartridges.
- Check with airline: antlers, skateboards, tents, umbrellas, fishing rods, bicycles.

Miscellaneous

Several items categorized by the TSA as miscellaneous items require special instructions to be brought on board or checked in luggage.

- Car engine parts and other car parts without fuel or traces of fuel are allowed in carry-on or checked bags. Car engine parts may be placed in checked bags only if the parts are packed in their original box and free of gasoline and oil.
- Cremated remains may be carried on board, but some airlines do not allow **cremated** remains in checked bags, so please check with your airline to learn more about possible restrictions. To facilitate screening, we suggest that you purchase a temporary or permanent crematory container made of a lighter weight material, such as wood or plastic. If the container is made of a material that generates an opaque image, TSA officers will not be able to clearly determine what is inside the container and the container will not be allowed. Out of respect for the deceased, TSA officers will not open a container, even if requested by the passenger.
- Musical instruments must undergo screening whether transported as carry-on or in checked bags. Inform the TSA officer if your instrument requires special care and handling. Pack brass instruments in your checked bags.

- Realistic toy guns are not allowed in carry-ons, but since the technology doesn't currently exist to create a real lightsaber, you can pack a toy lightsaber in your carry-on or checked bag.

- Parachutes should always be packed separately from other baggage. If a TSA officer determines that a bag must be opened to inspect the parachute, you must be present to assist in the inspection. If you are not within the screening area, you will be paged using the airport intercom system; if you are not present to assist with screening the parachute, the parachute will not be allowed on the plane. For this reason, passengers with parachutes are encouraged to add 30 minutes to the airlines' recommended arrival window. TSA is not responsible for repacking parachutes. All parachutes should be thoroughly inspected at their end destination to make sure that the equipment is still safe to use.

- Small pets are allowed through the checkpoint. Please check with your airline for their policy. Please remove your pet from the carrying case and place the case through the X-ray machine. You should maintain control of your pet with a leash and remember to remove the leash when carrying your pet through the metal detector. Animal carriers will undergo a visual and/or physical inspection.

Acceptable Miscellaneous Carry-ons

- For Babies And Children: carriers, seats, wipes, stuffed animals, snow globes, harry potter wand, glow sticks.

- For Adults: makeup and hair care products include hair pins, chapsticks, cologne, concealer, conditioner, dry shammpoo, hair clippers, hair dryer, hair gel, hair straightener (flat iron), hair texturizer, hairspray, jewelry, laser hair remover, nail polish, nail polish remover, powder makeup, shampoo, lipsticks, makeup remover, makeup wipes, mascara, mirrors, soap (bar), soap (liquid), solid makeup, perfume, tobacco, tobacco pipes, toothpaste, flowers, electronic toothbrushes, sunscreen sprays, wet wipes, foundation.

- Clothing: belts, clothes and shoes, shoe horn, shoe tree, blankets, body armor, handcuffs, steel-toed boots, electric blankets.

- Electronics and Hobbies: television, digital cameras, books, electronic cigarettes and vaping devices, binoculars, camera monopod, pens, putty balls, planting seeds, plants, headphones, Geiger counters, power charger, power inverters, tattoo inks, adult toys, artificial skeleton bones, shock collars, Xboxes, bread machine, car parts.

Banned Miscellaneous Items

- Banned From Checked Luggage: electronic cigarettes and vaping devices, live coral, live fish, power charger.
- Banned Completely: Replicas of explosives, such as hand grenades, fertilizer (note that handling fertilizer can cause a false positive on swab test).

Vocabulary

toll-free	[təul friː]	A toll-free telephone number is one which you can dial without having to pay for the call. *adj.* <美>（打电话）由接电话的机构付费的，受付 Donors can enjoy toll free blood use when they need it. 献血者在自己需要血液的时候可以享受全额免费。
prohibited	[prəˈhɪbɪtɪd]	If a law or someone in authority prohibits something, they forbid it or make it illegal. *v.* 禁止，阻止（prohibit 的过去式和过去分词）；不许 Smoking is strictly prohibited! 严禁吸咽！
aerosols	[ˈeərəsɒlz]	A metal container in which a liquid such as paint or hairspray is kept under pressure and released as a spray. *n.* （喷油漆、头发定型剂等的）喷雾器，雾化器；气雾剂；气溶胶 Hazardous materials include cleaning fluids, lighter fluid, and aerosols. 危险性物品包括清洁剂、轻液体和气雾剂。
facilitate	[fəˈsɪlɪteɪt]	To facilitate an action or process, especially one that you would like to happen, means to make it easier or more likely to happen. *v.* 促进；使便利 The new airport will facilitate the development of tourism. 新机场将促进旅游业的发展。
vapor	[ˈveɪpə(r)]	A visible suspension in the air of particles of some substance.

		n. 水蒸气
		The car windows were fogged with vapor. 车窗上满是雾气。
butane	['bjuːteɪn]	Butane is a gas that is obtained from petroleum and is used as a fuel.
		n. 丁烷
		Butane is found into both oil and natural gas. 丁烷气体是从石油和天然气中找到的。
chlorine	['klɔːriːn]	Chlorine is a strong-smelling gas that is used to clean water and to make cleaning products.
		n. 氯气
		Chlorine is used to disinfect water. 氯气用来给水消毒。
lithium	['lɪθiəm]	a chemical element. Lithium is a soft, very light, silver-white metal used in batteries and alloys.
		n. 锂
		The network will run for several weeks on AA size lithium batteries. 如果采用 5 号锂电池, 网络可运作数周之久。
miscellaneous	[ˌmɪsə'leɪniəs]	A miscellaneous group consists of many different kinds of things or people that are difficult to put into a particular category.
		adj. 各种各样的; 五花八门的; 混杂的; 多方面的
		They eat a lot of meats and dairy foods, along with a lot of miscellaneous items that don't fall into any group. 他们吃了大量的肉和奶制品, 还有许多不知道该归为什么类别的杂七杂八的东西。
cremated	['kriːˌmeɪtɪd]	When someone is cremated, their dead body is burned, usually as part of a funeral service.
		v. 焚烧, 火化 (尸体)
		v. 火葬, 火化 (尸体) (cremate 的过去式和过去分词)
		She wants Chris to be cremated. 她想把克里斯的尸体火化。

译文

机场随身行李安全规定

什么你可以携带或不可以携带

美国运输安全管理局（TSA）已经制定了一系列规则，规定了通过机场安全检查站的旅客在飞行时可以携带和不可以携带的物品。

新的安检政策会定期更新，包括允许和禁止登机的物品。

一般规则

TSA 规定，在飞行过程中您可以携带八类物品，无论是客舱里的随身行李，还是货舱里的托运行李。这份清单包括了适用于所有情况的规则，以及截至 2018 年 2 月 4 日被禁止的特定物品。

您可以携带的随身物品数量由各个航空公司确定：大多数航空公司规定您可以携带一件随身物品和一件私人物品。将您的随身物品整齐地分层包装，并将液体袋放在最上面。

飞机上根本不允许携带有害物质（HAZMAT）。违禁物品包括烹饪燃料、易爆物品，以及 FAA 规定的一些酒精含量高的饮料。

3-1-1 规则

根据 3-1-1 规则，液体、凝胶、乳膏、糊剂和气雾剂只能作为随身携带物品。任何容器不得超过 3.4 盎司（100 毫升）。旅行容器必须全部装入一个一夸脱大小的袋子中，并放在随身行李中，以方便安检。

3-1-1 规则的例外情况包括医疗必需的液体、药物和乳膏：您可以携带更多数量的医疗用品，并且不需要将它们放入塑料袋中。

但是，任何在扫描过程中引发警报的液体、气溶胶、凝胶、乳膏或糊状物都需要进行额外的检查。

易燃物

易燃物是任何很容易燃烧的物品。正如您想象的那样，其中许多被完全禁止带上飞机，但也有例外。

- 可接受的易燃随身物品：香烟、雪茄和安全火柴、一次性和 Zippo 打火机、手机充电器、移动电源、干电池、固体（但不是凝胶）蜡烛。
- 仅限托运的物品：彩虹火焰水晶、凝胶蜡烛和防身喷雾。
- 完全禁止的物品：任何易燃液体燃料，如烹饪燃料、丁烷、游泳池用氯气、爆竹、雷管和鞭炮。

锂电池的规则最近发生了重大变化。小于或等于 100 瓦的电池可以放在随身行李或托运行李中。托运行李中禁止携带松散的锂电池。

枪支

一般来说，TSA 不允许携带枪支或任何看起来或可能用作武器的东西。如果您符合枪支运输指南，则可以在托运行李中携带枪支，包括弹药、BB 枪、压缩空气枪、信号枪和枪支零件。从本质上讲，枪支必须卸载并放置在一个带锁的硬边容器中，该容器必须完全固定枪支。当您托运行李时，请务必告诉航空公司工作人员您正在托运枪支。

- 可随身携带物品：枪套、步枪瞄准镜、空弹壳。
- 仅限托运行李：弹药、BB 枪和压缩空气枪、枪支、信号枪、枪支零件、弹丸枪、逼真的复制品、步枪、弹壳、发令枪。
- 完全禁止：信号弹、手枪、打火机、火药。

食品

液体食品必须符合液体标准才能携带登机，但在大多数情况下，它们可以放在托运行李中。

肉类、海鲜、蔬菜和其他非流质食品都允许放入随身行李和托运行李中。如果食品用冰块或冰袋装在冷却器或其他容器中，则冰块或冰袋在通过扫描时必须完全冷冻。您可以将干冰和冷冻的易腐烂物品装入随身行李或托运行李中。FAA 允许您携带小于或等于 5 磅正确包装（包装有通风孔）并带有标记的干冰。

冷冻液体食品可以通过检查站，只要它们在接受检查时是已冷冻为固体。如果冷冻液体食品部分融化、变成浆状物或容器底部有任何液体，则它们必须满足 3-1-1 规则的液体要求。

允许将适量的水、配方奶粉、母乳和婴儿食品放在随身行李中；请参阅与儿童一起旅行的特殊说明。

- 可接受的随身携带食品：固体食品，如面包、糖果、谷物、咖啡豆；新鲜水果、肉类和蔬菜；鸡蛋、冷冻食品（如固态冷冻食品）、婴儿配方奶粉和食品。
- 仅限托运行李：不符合 3-1-1 规则的液体和奶油食品，如蜂蜜、肉汁、花生酱和奶油蘸酱。
- 完全禁止：酒精度超过 70%（140 美制酒度）的酒精饮料。

家庭用品

一般来说，家庭用品可以带上飞机，除非它们带有刀片或可以用作武器（斧头和搅拌机、牛刺、撬棍、烹饪喷雾、铸铁煎锅）。其中大部分可以放在托运行李中。

丁烷卷发棒等物品可以带上飞机，但不能带入货舱。电动工具和大于 7 英寸的常规工具禁止随身携带。液体物品（洗涤剂、除臭剂、洗手液）必须遵循 3-1-1 规则。

大多数笔记本电脑和手机可以带上飞机或放在托运行李中。三星 Galaxy Note 7 永久禁止在航空旅行中携带。

- 可接受的随身携带家庭物品（示例）：手机、计算机、绳状卷发器、咖啡机、洗涤剂、计算机、指尖陀螺、游戏机、笔记本电脑、灯泡、颜料、遥控车、收音机、缝纫机、订书机、文身枪。
- 仅限托运行李：斧头、钻头、锤子、加热垫、木槌、魔力八号球、射钉枪、电动工具和大于 7 英寸的工具。
- 禁止托运行李：丁烷卷发棒。
- 完全禁止：酒精含量超过 70%（140 美制酒度）的酒精饮料、烹饪喷雾、带有剩余燃料的发动机驱动设备、三星 Galaxy Note 7、溢出电池、喷雾淀粉、松节油和油漆稀释剂。

医疗用品

TSA 允许医疗用必需液体、凝胶和气雾剂不受 3-1-1 规则限制。您可以在旅途中携带合理数量的医疗用品，但您必须在检查站向 TSA 官员申报，以供检查。建议（但不要求）为您的药物贴上用于安全检查的标签：根据州法律确定标签的内容。用过的注射器装在锐器处理装置或其他类似的硬表面容器中运输是允许的。

如果调节阀未被篡改或拆除，则允许使用个人医用氧气瓶。允许携带但需要额外检查的物品：雾化器、CPAPs、BiPAPs、APAPs、未使用的注射器。如果您的身体里装有骨骼生长刺激器、脊柱刺激器、神经刺激器、端口、饲管、胰岛素泵、造口袋或其他医疗设备，您可能需要接受额外的检查。咨询设备制造商以确定它是否可以安全地通过 X 光机、金属探测器或先进的成像技术检查。

有关更多信息，请参阅 TSA 的残疾和医疗的规定。

- 可接受的随身医疗用品：血糖测试仪、手杖、石膏、隐形眼镜溶液、隐形眼镜、拐杖、EpiPens、特殊的外部医疗设备、眼药水、吸入器、胰岛素、胰岛素泵和用品、救生衣、液体维生素、液体药物、药丸、硝酸甘油药丸、药丸切割器、假肢、补充剂、支撑支架、温度计、未使用的注射器、维生素、助行器和轮椅。
- 完全禁止：随身携带或托运行李中禁止携带医用大麻。

尖锐物品

一般情况下，您的随身行李中禁止携带尖锐物品，但可以装在您的托运行李中。托运行李中的尖锐物品应被覆盖或牢固包裹，以防止对行李搬运工和安检员造成伤害。

- 可随身携带的锋利物品：雪茄剪、钩针、一次性剃须刀、织针、指甲钳、卷笔刀、安全别针、距离轴点不到 4 英寸的剪刀、缝纫针、镊子。

- 仅限托运行李：开瓶器、开箱刀、冰镐和斧头、刀具、皮革工具、切肉刀、小刀、剃须刀、军刀、带刀片的安全剃须刀、锯、瑞士军刀、剑、飞星。

运动和露营设备

运动和露营设备通常可以随身携带，但下列物品除外：归为危险品的物品，如一些气雾杀虫剂、可用作武器的物品、不符合 3-1-1 规则的液体、航空公司规定的超大物品。

露营炉具只有在已清空所有燃料并进行清洁以确保没有燃料蒸气或残留物时，才允许放在随身携带行李或托运行李中。请将绳索和物品分别包裹放在袋子里，以便工作人员可以清楚地看到物品。您可以携带一件救生衣，里面最多装有两个氧气瓶，并在您的随身行李或托运行李中携带两个备用氧气瓶。

可能被视为危险物品的锋利渔具，例如大鱼钩，应套上护套、牢固包裹并装入托运行李中。与其他高价值物品一样，您可能希望您的随身行李中的昂贵胶卷或易碎物品能被安全运输。

- 可接受的随身携带运动物品：棒球、篮球、足球、地掷球、保龄球、自行车链条和打气筒、拳击手套、冷藏箱、除草工具、钓鱼竿和钓竿、橄榄球头盔、高尔夫球、高尔夫球 T 恤、暖手器、头盔、长板、GPS 导航、软弹枪、岩石、沙子、溜冰鞋、睡袋、小鱼饵、滑雪板、雪鞋、运动夹板、网球拍、奖杯、真空密封袋。
- 仅限托运的物品：棒球棒、保龄球瓶、弓箭、独木舟/皮划艇桨、铸铁炊具、冰爪、板球棒、高尔夫球杆、登山杖、曲棍球棒、长曲棍球棒、武术武器、双节棍、台球杆、鞋钉和雪钉、滑雪杖、雪夹板、矛枪、帐篷钉、手杖。
- 完全禁止物品：烟花爆竹、小型压缩弹药筒。
- 向航空公司查询确认的物品：鹿角、滑板、帐篷、雨伞、钓竿、自行车。

杂项

一些被 TSA 归类为杂项的物品需要特殊说明才能带上飞机或托运。

- 汽车发动机部件和其他不含燃料或微量燃料的汽车部件可放入随身行李或托运行李中。仅当汽车发动机部件装在原包装箱中且不含汽油和机油时，才可以将其放入托运行李中。
- 骨灰可以带上飞机，但一些航空公司不允许将骨灰放在托运行李中，因此请与您的航空公司联系以了解更多可能的限制。为便于检查，我们建议您购买由重量较轻的材料（如木材或塑料）制成的临时或永久性火葬容器。如果容器由产生不透明图像的材料制成，TSA 官员将无法清楚地确定容器内是什么，那么容器将不被允许带上飞机。出于对死者的尊重，即使乘客提出要求，TSA 官员也不会打开容器。

- 乐器无论是随身携带还是托运，都必须经过检查。如果您的乐器需要特别小心护理和处理，请通知 TSA 官员。将铜管乐器放入托运行李中。
- 逼真的玩具枪不允许随身携带，但由于目前尚不存在制造真正光剑的技术，因此您可以将玩具光剑装入随身行李或托运行李中。
- 降落伞应始终与其他行李分开包装。如果 TSA 官员确定必须打开一个袋子来检查降落伞，您必须在场协助检查。如果您不在安检区域内，工作人员会使用机场对讲系统呼叫；如果您不在场协助检查降落伞，降落伞将不被允许带上飞机。出于这个原因，我们建议带降落伞的乘客按照航空公司建议到达窗口时间再提前 30 分钟。TSA 不负责重新包装降落伞。所有降落伞都应在其最终目的地进行彻底检查，以确保装备仍然可以安全使用。
- 小宠物可以通过检查站。请咨询您的航空公司了解相关的政策。请将您的宠物从手提箱中取出，然后将手提箱通过 X 光机。您应该用皮带保持对宠物的控制，并记住在携带宠物通过金属探测器时取下皮带。动物携带者将接受 X 光机检查或人工检查。

可接受的杂项随身行李

- 婴儿和儿童：背带、座椅、湿巾、毛绒动物玩具、雪球、哈利波特魔杖、荧光棒。
- 成人：化妆和护发用品，包括发夹、唇膏、古龙香水、遮瑕膏、护发素、干洗发水、理发剪、吹风机、发胶、直发器（扁铁）、头发定型剂、发胶、珠宝、激光脱毛剂、指甲油、卸甲油、粉妆、洗发水、口红、卸妆液、化妆湿巾、睫毛膏、镜子、香皂（条）、香皂（液体）、固体化妆品、香水、烟草、烟斗、牙膏、鲜花、电动牙刷、防晒霜喷雾、湿巾、粉底。
- 服装：腰带、衣服和鞋子、鞋拔、鞋撑、毛毯、防弹衣、手铐、钢头靴、电热毯。
- 电子产品和个人喜好用品：电视、数码相机、书籍、电子烟和电子烟设备、双筒望远镜、相机独脚架、钢笔、油灰球、种植种子、植物、耳机、盖革计数器、充电器、电源逆变器、文身墨水、成人玩具、人造骨架骨骼、减震项圈、可视化游戏键盘控制台、面包机、汽车零件。

违禁杂项物品

- 禁止托运行李：电子烟和电子烟设备、活珊瑚、活鱼、充电器。
- 完全禁止：炸药的复制品，如手榴弹、肥料（注意处理肥料会导致拭子测试呈假阳性）。

ⓡeading Material

How to Know What You Can and Can't Carry on Board an Aircraft

Increasing airport security regulations are making it more and more difficult to know what can and can't be carried on board an aircraft. You may leave a country with your gel pack, only to have it confiscated upon return. This article provides you guidelines for staying informed and minimizing the risks of losing something to security, being subjected to additional screening, missing your flight, or ending up in trouble.

Method 1　Be Informed

Know which organization you may need to be in contact with. Keep a list with their websites and phone numbers handy while travelling. Useful organizations include:

- the bureau of consular affairs;
- transportation security administration;
- the airline(s) you are travelling with.

Method 2　Know the Basics

1

Know the 3-1-1 rule. For travel in the US, a passenger is allowed in their carry-on no more than a maximum of 3 bottles containing no more than 3.4 ounces (100 ml) liquid. Bottles must be placed in a quart-sized, clear plastic, zip-top bag.

2

Rethink packing potentially problematic items. Certain items that are generally permitted may still be subject to additional screening or prohibited at security's discretion (such as if it triggers an alarm or appears to have been tampered with). Items that can potentially pose security concerns include:

- sharp objects;
- sporting goods;
- tools;
- firearms and martial arts weapons;
- foods including creamy dips, jams, and salsa;
- liquid contain decorative items such as lava lamps or snow globes;
- cannabis, even if it is legal in your state/country.

3

Always take prescriptions with your medication, and try to carry on medications in their original packaging. This will not only enable you to carry the item on the aircraft with you, it will also assist with any questions a customs officer might raise in your country of arrival.

4

Play it safe. If you are unsure about an item, mail it ahead of time or leave it at home.

Method 3   Be Prepared and Aware

1

Know what you have. You are responsible for your belongings and what's in them, so double-check pockets and compartments of clothing and bags for items that may have been forgotten about such as lighters, swiss-army knives, bottle openers, etc.

2

Be aware that the list of prohibited items is constantly being updated, especially when there is a security scare. Refer to the relevant websites to find out immediately before travelling what restrictions are in place.

3

Declare larger quantities of liquids. There may be exemptions for certain items such as medications, baby formula, breast milk, and certain foods. You can declare these items but should know that officers may need to conduct additional screening which can take longer.

Tips

Check the TSA website frequently for a list of what you can and can't bring.

Arrive at the airport and check through security early enough to ensure time to repack or mail belongings that security may have issue with.

Use common sense and do not carry anything that is obviously illegal or intended for use as a weapon or a fire starter (including matches).

If you feel faint or ill during the bustle of the screening process, let somebody know immediately. Deep breathing is a big asset in times of stress and long waits.

If in doubt, leave it, mail it, or pack it in your cargo baggage.

Don't expect to be compensated for lost items. If the item is valuable, make sure it is insured in case of loss.

It is okay to carry AA & AAA batteries on board.

If you are travelling with a child (or even yourself) it may be a good idea to bring gum or chewy sweets for when you are going for lift off because of ear popping.

Warnings

Avoid making any jokes about guns, bombs, terrorism, weapons, knives, stabbings, murders, suffocation, crime, illegal/illicit conduct, inefficiency of TSA, or anything else that could be taken as a threat.

Airport security views safety issues very seriously and will not tolerate people behaving badly. Try to be patient and understanding and don't argue, make a fuss, or throw a temper tantrum.

Never make a joke about having prohibited items. Airport security is required to take such statements seriously.

You are responsible for what's in your bags, so keep an eye on your belongings at all times and know what's inside of them. Keep an eye on children's packing and make sure you know what they have packed.

**xercises**

1. Vocabulary

(1) Smoking is strictly (   ).

    A. incited   B. commended   C. allowed   D. prohibited

(2) Hazardous materials include cleaning fluids, lighter fluid and (   ).

A. glue   B. aerosols   C. yogurt   D. soda water

(3) The network will run for several weeks on AA size (   ) batteries.

A. lithium   B. zinc   C. lead   D. copper

(4) Influence of Aging Process on Performance and Structure of Catalyst for (   ) Oxidation.

A. Chlorine   B. Nitrogen   C. Butane   D. Oxygen

(5) The car windows were fogged with (   ).

A. vapor   B. water   C. ice   D. mud

2. Dialogue

(1) O: Excuse me,（你身上还有其他的金属物品吗？）

P: No. My pockets are empty.

(2) O:（请脱下您的鞋，走到那边。请站在这个台子上。）Your shoes should be x-rayed separately.

P: But, is the floor clean?

O: Don't worry.（垫子是消过毒的。）Now hold out your arms and stand with your feet apart please.

3. Translate

（1）您可以将液体、气溶胶和凝胶放在机舱行李中，只要每个物品的最大体积不超过 100 毫升，装在一个可重新密封的透明塑料袋中，每个乘客可携带的容量不超过 1 升。

（2）在美国和澳大利亚/新西兰，对运输某些类型的粉末进入飞机舱有安全限制，将最大体积限制在 350 毫升（12 盎司）。

（3）您可以在手提行李中携带在免税商店购买的任何数量的液体、气溶胶和凝胶物品，只要您保留购买证明并保存在一个密封的、防篡改的袋子中。

（4）有限数量的药品、洗漱用品和酒精饮料可放在托运行李或舱内行李中（最多 2 升或 2 千克）。

（5）联盟航空公司保留决定哪些物品不安全而不能运输的权利，因为这些物品是危险的，不安全的，或者因为它们的重量、大小、形状或特点，或者它们是易碎的或易腐蚀的物品。

 **ialogue**

Checking the Carry-on Baggage

Dialogue 1

O: Excuse me, but is this your bag?

P: Yes.

O: I need you to open your bag and check the items.

P: Of course, you can check my bag.

O: You can't take liquids through the security, so I will have to take the bottle of water away.

P: Oh, I forgot all about it.

O: That's OK. It happens all the time. There is nothing else in your bag that I need to remove. You can go now.

P: Thank you.

Dialogue 2

O: Is this your bag? I must open it for a further check.

(a moment later)

O: What is inside these small bottles?

P: They are bottles of makeup.

O: We need to open them to check inside of each.

P: No, they are gifts for my friends. I don't want to open them.

O: Then you will need to return to the counter and check-in your baggage. They are not permitted to be taken on board according to the new regulations.

P: OK. I will go to the check-in counter.

O: Thanks for your cooperation.

Dialogue 3

O: Is this your bag?

P: Yes.

O: I must open it for a further check.

P: OK.

O: What's this?

P: It is a small Swiss Army knife.

O: Sorry, it is not permitted to be taken on board according to the Civil Aviation Law of China.

P: Oh, what should I do with it?

O: You need to return to the counter and put it into your checked baggage.

P: But I haven't any checked baggage.

O: If you do not want to lose it, there is a post counter where you can have it mailed to your destination.

P: I am in a hurry. I do not have time to return to the post counter. I guess I will have to abandon it.

O: Sorry but that is the policy. Thanks for your cooperation.

Text

Open Architecture Could Benefit Airport Security

Regulators and airport operators from across Europe, North America, Asia-Pacific and the Middle East say they have joined forces to promote the introduction of open architecture in airport security systems.

In a recently published paper, prepared by Heathrow Airport Limited and Avinor AS and **endorsed** by a wide range of regulators and airport **stakeholders**, the authors and **collaborators** state that a safe and secure aviation system is the foundation of the global economy.

It notes that the security threat to this system is real and continues to evolve, with technology changing the way the world and those with **malicious** intent operate. The document sets out broad **guidelines** for how airport security systems can share data and how airports can work with partners, provides a path forward for new, innovative software developers to help defeat **terrorism**.

TSA administrator David Pekoske, Heathrow Airport CEO John Holland-Kaye and ACI Europe director general Olivier Jankovec said, "The key to our success is the shared ability to **collaborate** across the public, private and **academic** sectors. It is through these partnerships that we bring the best technologies and brightest minds together and rise to the collective challenge of outmatching a **dynamic** threat."

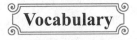

architecture	[ˈɑːkɪtektʃə(r)]	the design and structure of a computer system
		n. 体系结构；（总体、层次）结构，建筑学；建筑风格；建筑式样；架构
		In this architecture, all data for each vertex must be available at the same time. 在这一架构中，来自各顶点的所有数据都必须同时可用。

endorse	[ɪn'dɔːs]	to say publicly that you support a person, statement or course of action *vt.*（公开）赞同，支持，认可，背书；签署 I can endorse their opinion wholeheartedly. 我可以全心全意地支持他们的观点。
stakeholder	['steɪkhəʊldə(r)]	a person or company that is involved in a particular organization, project, system, etc, especially because they have invested money in it *n.*（某组织、工程、体系等的）参与人，参与方；有权益关系者，利益相关者；赌金保管者 复数 stakeholders The government has said it wants to create a stakeholder economy in which all members of society feel that they have an interest in its success. 政府表示希望建立一种人人参与的经济模式，让社会全体成员觉得其繁荣将给每个人带来利益。
collaborator	[kə'læbəreɪtə(r)]	a person who works with another person to create or produce sth such as a book *n.* [劳经] 合作者；协作者；合著者 复数 collaborators The Irvine group and their collaborators are testing whether lasers do the job better. 欧文小组和他们的合作者们正在测试是否用激光更好。
malicious	[mə'lɪʃəs]	having or showing hatred and a desire to harm sb or hurt their feelings *adj.* 恶意的；恶毒的；蓄意的；怀恨的 That might merely have been malicious gossip. 那可能只是恶意闲言。
guideline	['gaɪdlaɪnz]	If an organization issues guidelines on something, it issues official advice about how to do it. *n.* 指导方针 The government should issue clear guidelines on the content of religious education. 政府应该颁布明确的关于宗教教育内容的指导方针。
terrorism	['terərɪzəm]	The use of violent action in order to achieve political

aims or to force a government to act.

n. 恐怖主义；恐怖行动；恐怖统治

The government is taking a firm line on terrorism. 政府现在对恐怖主义采取强硬的态度。

collaborate	[kə'læbəreɪt]	to work together with sb in order to produce or achieve sth *vi.* 合作 Researchers around the world are collaborating to develop a new vaccine. 世界各地的研究人员正在合作培育一种新的疫苗。
academic	[ˌækə'demɪk]	involving a lot of reading and studying rather than practical or technical skills *adj.* 学术的（与实践性、技术性相对）；理论的；学院的 It is a purely academic question. 这是一个纯理论问题。
dynamic	[daɪ'næmɪk]	the way in which people or things behave and react to each other in a particular situation *adj.* （人或事物）相互作用的方式，动态，动态的；动力的 The dynamic adjustment to low oil prices may, however, be different this time around. 然而，这次对低油价的动态调整可能有所不同。

译文

开放式架构有利于机场安全

来自欧洲、北美、亚太和中东的监管机构人员和机场运营商表示，他们已联手推动在机场安全系统中引入开放式架构。

在最近发表的由希思罗机场有限公司和阿维诺编写并得到监管机构和机场利益相关者广泛认可的论文中，作者和合作者指出，安全可靠的航空系统是全球经济的基础。

该论文指出，随着技术改变了世界和恶意用户的操作，该系统的安全威胁是真实存在的，并在不断演变。该论文为机场安全系统如何共享数据以及机场如何与合作伙伴合作提供了广泛的指导方针，为新的创新软件开发人员提供了一条前进的道路，以帮助他们击败恐怖主义。

运输安全管理局局长大卫·佩科斯克、希思罗机场首席执行官约翰·霍兰德·凯伊和 ACI 欧洲总监奥利维尔·扬科维奇表示："我们成功的关键是公共、运营和技术部门之间的协作能力。正是通过这些伙伴关系，我们将最好的技术和最聪明的人才聚集在一起，共同应对挑战，战胜动态的威胁。"

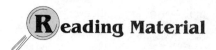

How to Pack to Get Through Airport Security Fast

Airport security can take a long time to move through, especially if your bag is disorganized or improperly packed. To avoid bag searches and maximize efficiency, carefully consider what you do and do not need. When packing, place the objects least likely to be searched on the bottom with laptops and liquids near the top. Investing in a good bag can also help you move quickly through security.

Method 1 Bringing What You Need

1

Check a bag. A checked bag will allow you to bring more with you, and you will have to carry less in your carry-on. Put as much as you can in the checked bag instead of your carry-on. The less you bring in your carry-on, the less likely you are to be pulled for a bag search.

Clothing, toiletries, and souvenirs can all be packed in a checked-bag.

Pack books in a checked bag unless you are planning on reading them on the plane.

Electronics, like cameras and laptops, and valuable possessions, like jewelry, should always be packed in a carry-on.

2

Pack only what you need. You should only put necessities in your carry-on. If you have too much in the bag, the security agents may not be able to use the X-ray properly, and it can increase your chances of being stopped for a bag search. Things you need may include:

phone;

laptop/tablet;

camera;

charger;

magazine or book for the plane;

medication;

food or milk for young children;

extra set of clothing in case your checked bag is lost.

3

Lay out what you are packing. Before you pack your carry-on, lay out everything that you are planning to bring. You can do this on a bed, desk, or table. This will allow you to see if you are bringing too much, and it will help you organize your belongings in the most efficient fashion. It can also help you notice if you forgot anything.

When laying things out, keep similar things together. For example, stack all of your clothes together while placing any chargers with their appropriate electronics.

Make sure that you have your ID, passport (if travelling internationally), and ticket ready to go.

4

Double-check for prohibited items. Some objects can only be checked on an airplane while others are prohibited entirely. Always double-check that you are not bringing these items onto the plane. If you are caught with one of them, you may be delayed.

Bleach, lighter fluid, gasoline, aerosol cans, or any other flammable or explosive material are all forbidden from planes.

Weapons (like guns, Tasers, and knives), sporting equipment (like baseball bats, golf clubs, or ski poles), and electronic cigarettes must all be placed in a checked bag.

5

Avoid large objects. Big, oddly shaped items are not technically prohibited, but they can get your bag pulled from the X-ray for a manual search. If you must bring items like this, pack them in a checked bag, or remove them before going through security. Some things you may want to watch out for include:

large electronics, like X boxes, portable DVD players, or CPAP machines;

bulky books, manuals, or dictionaries;

large crystals like geodes;

dense metallic objects.

Method 2　Arranging Your Luggage

1

Pack clothing on the bottom. If you are packing clothing in your carry-on, you should fold or roll each item. Place clothing on the bottom of your bag. If you have any other items that you will not need until you land, place them with the clothing.

2

Put your liquids in a plastic bag. Even if your local airport offers plastic bags, you should pack your own liquids ahead of time. Find a one-quart clear plastic bag. Containers for liquids must be no larger than 3.4 ounces or 100 ml, and they must fit into the plastic bag.

If the containers are larger than 3.4 ounces, they must be placed in a checked bag, even if the amount of liquid inside is less than that amount.

Instead of buying travel sized versions of your toiletries, you can purchase reusable travel-sized bottles. Fill these up at home with your favorite shampoo, conditioner, soap, and other toiletries.

3

Place electronics and liquids on top. Laptops and liquids must be removed when going through security. To remove these as quickly as possible, place these items at the top of your bag. Make sure that they are easy to access so that you can pull them out quickly.

4

Stick documents and money in the outside pockets. You will need to have your documents and wallet handy. They cannot be placed in your pockets as you go through security. Put your wallet and documents in an outer pocket of your luggage. You can pull out your ID and ticket when you need it to go through security.

If you are bringing a purse or briefcase as an extra personal item, you can put your ID and ticket in there, but make sure that you can pull it out quickly. You do not want to have to rummage through your bag to find your ticket.

5

Organize everything neatly. Well-organized bags allow security to look through your bag quickly on the X-ray. When placing items in your bag, make sure that they are neatly stacked and arranged.

Clothing should be folded. You can buy packing cubes to help keep clothing from crumpling in your bag.

Wind up chargers, and stick them next to the electronics.

Books should be stacked together.

Large electronics such as laptops must be removed before being placed in the X-ray. If you place the electronics near the top of your bag, you can quickly remove them without messing up the rest of your luggage.

Method 3　Choosing the Right Bag

1

Measure the bag. Airlines have specific regulations for how large your carry-on bag can be. If your bag is too big, it may be stopped at security or at the gate. Check with your airline to see what their size limit is, and measure your bag to make sure it will fit.

While each airline may have its own regulations, most limit you to a piece of luggage that is 45 linear inches or about 115 linear centimeters. This means that the total height, width, and length of the bag equals either 45 inches or 115 centimeters.

You should always measure a bag before buying. Just because the label says that it is carry-on compliant doesn't mean that it is.

2

Look for a TSA compliant laptop bag. A TSA compliant laptop bag should have a separate laptop compartment. If you put the laptop in this sleeve, you will not have to remove it when going through the X-ray. Nothing else can be put in this compartment. The computer's mouse and charger must be kept in a different pocket.

3

Bring a small personal item. Most airlines will allow you bring on a small personal item with your carry-on. These can give you extra space to pack. If they are large enough, you can put your liquids, documents, wallet, and laptop in this personal item, and keep items that do not need to be searched in your larger carry-on bag. Common personal items include:

purse;

laptop bag;

briefcase.

Tips

In the US, you can apply for TSA Pre-Check. If approved, you can move through security in a special lane without removing your liquids or electronics.

Always double-check that you have your ID or passport with you before you leave for the airport.

Do not wear jewelry or other metal objects through security. Wearing slip-on shoes can also help reduce the amount of time you take when going through.

Warnings

Do not attempt to sneak sharp or flammable items onto the plane.

There is no guarantee that you will not be pulled for a random bag search while going through airport security. Make sure you arrive with plenty of time before your flight.

Exercises

1. Vocabulary

(1) In this (   ), all data for each vertex must be available at the same time.

    A. building   B. architecture   C. framework   D. structure

(2) I can (   ) their opinion wholeheartedly.

    A. endorse   B. hold   C. approve   D. sign

(3) The government is taking a firm line on (   ).

    A. danger   B. terror   C. terrifying   D. terrorism

(4) Researchers around the world are (   ) to develop a new vaccine.

    A. merging   B. collaborating   C. coordinating   D. combinating

(5) The (   ) adjustment to low oil prices may, however, be different this time around.

    A. dynamic   B. active   C. mobile   D. removed

2. Dialogue

(1) O:（请打开您的包接受检查。）

    P: Of course you can check my bag.

(2) O: Is this your bag? （我必须进一步检查。）

    O:（这些小瓶子里是什么东西？）

P: They are bottles of makeup.

3. Translate

(1) Dangerous goods are items or substances that may endanger the safety of an aircraft, passengers or cargo on board.

(2) The Transportation Security Administration is giving its airport checkpoint officers a new tool: a kit to test for explosive powders.

(3) If the X-ray machine detects a potentially hazardous powder, a sample will be mixed with a solution for testing.

(4) Travelers can still board planes with powders such as baby formula, makeup and medicines.

(5) The majority of passengers won't notice any difference in checkpoint procedures, this is just one additional layer of security that helps bolster our explosive detection capability.

 ialogue

Patrolling in the Airport Terminal Sterile Area

Dialogue 1

O: Whose baggage is this?

P: It's mine.

O: It is the policy that unattended baggage be confiscated. You must keep them with you at all times.

P: Sorry, I will be more careful. Thank you for letting me know.

Dialogue 2

P: Excuse me, sir.

O: Yes. How can I help you?

P: My flight will depart at Gate B25. Would you please tell me how to get there?

O: Please go straight and turn left in 100 meters. Gate B25 is at the end of the corridor.

P: Excuse me, it is my first time flying. How can I find the gate?

O: It will be easy to find. Each gate is clearly marked.

P: I see. Thank you very much.

O: My pleasure.

Dialogue 3

O: Excuse me. You are not allowed to wait here.

P: Oh, but I'm waiting for my wife. The officer is checking her baggage over there now.

O: Yes, I understand, but for reasons of security you need to keep walking. The sign clearly says that you cannot wait here. Don't worry, your wife will be able to join you.

P: Oh, I'm sorry. I'll leave here at once.

O: Thank you very much.

Text

The Technology Ushering in a New Era of Airport Security

When it comes to the airport passenger journey, the security screening process is typically seen as one of the most stressful points. With the removal of shoes, belts and **jewellery**, having to separate belongings into trays, and taking electronics and liquids out of bags, queues tend to build, and so does passenger impatience. For this reason, the **application** of advanced technologies at the checkpoint has been a priority for airports in a bid to create or maintain a competitive advantage. This priority has become an imperative in a world with coronavirus, with the need to rebuild confidence in air travel and increase operational efficiency by creating a seamless flow of passengers through security while **minimising** all contact points.

That's where computer tomography (CT) comes in. Typically employed in the medical sector, CT technology **generates** 3D, volumetric X-ray images. In the context of airport security, CT scanners enable security operators to inspect baggage from every angle. Automatic explosives detection algorithms and automated object recognition software, which can detect prohibited items such as weapons, support operators in making fast and accurate decisions. This not only **boosts** operational efficiency, but also the security **outcome**.

The growing **adoption** of this technology around the globe is great news for passengers, with CT scanners eliminating the need to take liquids and electronic devices out of luggage, drastically cutting queuing times and creating a more **frictionless** experience at the checkpoint.

In the US for example, the Transportation Security Administration (TSA) is working to implement CT technology, and recently Miami International Airport unveiled seven Smiths Detection CTiX scanners installed at TSA checkpoints, allowing passengers to keep laptops and electronic devices in their carry-on bags to minimise touch points during the screening process.

However, CT scanners also support the enhanced health and safety measures implemented at airports, by minimising touch points. With automatic detection capabilities and low false alarm rates, unnecessary interaction between passengers and operators is reduced and physical distancing amongst travellers can be more easily implemented with quicker screening. With liquids and laptops being allowed to remain in bags during screening, the number of trays handled by both staff and passengers is drastically reduced.

CT scanners can certainly help airports address critical issues faced by COVID-19, but what about the unknown threats of the future? Checkpoint enhancements must still be geared towards maximising security to most effectively address emerging crime, terrorist and biological threats, while optimising passenger experience. The self-service, fully automated checkpoint of the future is the ideal, and CT scanners play a crucial role in turning this concept into a reality. At Smiths Detection we are committed to **harnessing** the advanced detection performance of our CT technology to enhance our algorithmic automatic object recognition software even further. This could enable alarm-only viewing of X-ray images to create a contactless and highly efficient security process.

Vocabulary

usher	[ˈʌʃə(r)]	to take or show sb where they should go vt. 把……引往；引导，招待；迎接；开辟 That widget alone could usher in a whole new area of interactive television. 仅此一项，我们认为交互式电视就被引入一个全新的领域。
jewellery	[ˈdʒuːəlri]	objects such as rings and necklaces that people wear as decoration n. 珠宝；首饰（等于 jewelry） Discover a full selection of fine watches and jewellery

at these two Upper Manhattan stores. 在这两家上曼哈顿区的商店里找到全套精品手表和珠宝。

application	[ˌæplɪ'keɪʃn]	(of sth) (to sth) the practical use of sth, especially a theory, discovery, etc *n.* （尤指理论、发现等的）应用，运用；申请 The invention would have wide application in industry. 这项发明会在工业中得到广泛应用。
minimise	['mɪnɪmaɪz]	to reduce sth, especially sth bad, to the lowest possible level *vt.* 使减少到最低限度，使减到最少 Good hygiene helps to minimise the risk of infection. 保持清洁有助于最大限度地减少感染的危险。
generate	['dʒenəreɪt]	to produce or create sth *vt.* 产生；引起，使形成；发生 Emotional upsets generate powerful and deadly toxic substances. 情绪的不安会产生强大而致命的有毒物质。
boost	[buːst]	to make sth increase, or become better or more successful *vt.* 使增长；使兴旺，促进；增加 The movie helped boost her screen career. 那部电影有助于她的银幕生涯的发展。
outcome	['aʊtkʌm]	the result or effect of an action or event *n.* 结果；效果，结局；成果 复数 outcomes We are confident of a successful outcome. 我们相信会有圆满的结果。
adoption	[ə'dɒpʃn]	the decision to start using sth such as an idea, a plan or a name *n.* （想法、计划、名字等的）采用 The group is working to promote the adoption of broadband wireless access over long distances. 该集团正在致力于推广远距离宽带无线访问的采用。
friction	['frɪkʃn]	the action of one object or surface moving against another

frictionless		*n.* 摩擦，[力] 摩擦力 *adj.* 无摩擦的；光滑的 Friction between moving parts had caused the engine to overheat. 活动部件的摩擦使发动机过热。 A perpetual motion machine would have to be frictionless. 永动机只能是一种无摩擦力的机器。
harness	['hɑːnɪs]	to control and use the force or strength of sth to produce power or to achieve sth *v.* 控制，利用（以产生能量等），治理，利用 Turkey plans to harness the waters of the Tigris and Euphrates rivers for big hydro-electric power projects. 土耳其计划利用底格里斯河与幼发拉底河的水来建造大型水力发电工程。

译文

开启机场安全新技术时代

对于乘客在机场的登机流程，安检流程通常被视为最紧张的环节之一。随着脱鞋子、解下腰带、摘下首饰，把随身物品分别放入托盘中，把电子产品和液体从包中取出，排队的人数越来越多，乘客也越来越不耐烦。因此，在安检流程中应用先进技术已成为机场创造和保持竞争优势的优先事项。随着新冠肺炎病毒在全世界的肆虐，需要重建对航空旅行的信心并提高运营效率，实现安检乘客的无缝流动，同时最大限度地减少所有接触点，这一优先事项成为当务之急。

安检成为计算机断层摄影（CT）的用武之地。CT 技术通常用于医疗领域，可生成3D 立体 X 射线图像。在机场安检过程，安检人员使用 CT 扫描仪能够从各个角度检查行李。通过自动爆炸物检测算法和自动物体识别软件，可以检测到武器等违禁物品，支持安检人员做出快速准确的判断。这不仅可以提高运营效率，还可以提高安全性。

这项技术在全球广泛采用对乘客来说是个好消息，CT 扫描仪免除了从行李中取出液体和电子设备的要求，大大缩短了排队时间，创造了更加顺畅的安检体验。

例如，在美国，运输安全管理局（TSA）正在努力实施 CT 技术，最近迈阿密国际机场推出了安装在 TSA 检查站的七台史密斯检测 CTiX 扫描仪，允许乘客将笔记本电脑和电子设备放在随身行李中，尽量减少筛查过程中的接触。

不管怎样，CT 扫描仪也通过减少接触点使机场的健康和安全措施更有效。凭借自动检测功能和低误报率，减少了乘客和操作员之间不必要的互动，并且可以通过旅客之间保持一定距离，减少身体接触来实现更快、更轻松的安检。由于允许在安检期间过程中将液体和笔记本电脑放在行李中，工作人员和乘客处理托盘的数量会明显减少。

CT 扫描仪肯定可以帮助机场解决新冠肺炎疫情的关键问题，但未来的未知威胁呢？检查站的改进仍必须面向最大限度地提高安全性，以最有效地应对新出现的犯罪、恐怖主义和生物威胁，同时优化乘客体验。未来的自助式全自动检查站是理想之选，而 CT 扫描仪在将这一概念变为现实方面发挥着至关重要的作用。对于史密斯检测扫描仪，我们致力于利用 CT 技术的先进检测性能来进一步改进算法自动对象识别软件。这可以在查看 X 射线图像时启用报警技术，以创建非接触式、高效的安检流程。

eading Material

How to Navigate from the 12 Terminals to the Boarding Gate at Orlando International Airport (MCO)

If you've ever been to Orlando before, you've potentially flown out of or through Orlando International Airport. Once you get inside the airport doors, navigating its long hallways and corridors makes things confusing. This article can explain how to navigate this airport so things seem less tricky and get you to your gate without any major disasters occurring.

1

Arrive at the entrance to the terminals. Pick up your tickets from the ticketing agents if you don't have them just yet, or if your smartphone isn't able to provide them to you, or if you don't have access to these tickets. You'll need them to pass through the TSA lines later on.

2

Walk down the hallway until you see a turn-in that has a humongous and airy (tall) roomed area. You'll be on the third level of the airport. This area will have several display monitors that tell you your gate assignment for your flight if the flight's information has changed since your tickets were printed or some other factor changed the flight pattern or flight gate.

3

Follow through this open and airy area until you notice the TSA lines. The TSA lines tend to be very long here, but if you have all your stuff handy and out, you don't have to reach in and can get through. Listen to the TSA agents as you walk through the aisles. These aisles will get you to the checked baggage lanes.

4

Place all your baggage on the belt, including all metal items and jackets. Be sure to include your sneakers/shoes, phones, wallets, anything that is loose.

Although belts don't tend to trigger problems, be sure your belt comes off.

Place any loose items into a plastic square bin that is found off the edge of the rolling racks before the item's X-ray machines.

5

Walk up to and into the full-body scanners. These body scanners are of the newest variety. Walk into them and turn to your right. Look at the picture. Hold your hands open and form in the shape of a curved V (almost as if you were forming them into an almost interconnected valentine heart well above your head.) Wait for the machine to X-ray you. Most people pass through the machine without much interruption.

These newest scanners beginning the 100% screening were installed in 2007 following a firearms and marijuana smuggling case discovered at this airport.

6

Continue walking on the path. Look at the large numbered signs above your head that lead you to the monorail/shuttle-to-gates. Once you start to see several square-tube like items with a circular plastic piece (that may or may not have a fluorescent light that designates these transportation devices), make sure that the alleyway sends you to the gate containing your flight.

7

Be sure to check the gate boards right outside the monorail to ensure you travel to the gate area containing your specific gate.

8

Travel on the shuttle and take the monorail to the flight gates. With the exception at the end of each monorail car, there are no seats in the monorail. Everybody must stand. Be prepared for a few-minute shuttle to the gate area.

Don't go too far down the alleyway if you'd like to go forward and be able to sit. The best place to sit (and rarely crowded) is the seat at the monorail's very back. The other monorail cars will tend to be crowded and almost always have no seats going in the forward direction or no seats whatsoever.

Exit from the monorail car through the doors that open once the monorail stops. The doors that open should be the opposite sided ones than those you entered through the last time.

9

Walk past the end of the monorail/shuttle and down the ramp that leads you into the airport gates. Find your gate and sit down.

10

Look up at the TV displays at the gate to ensure that your plane (flight number) is still available to be boarded from that exact gate. Most often, no other changes are needed, as most flights don't change gates that often. But be prepared if your flight changes gates.

Tips

The third floor is set up for departures and arrivals. The second is set up for baggage claim. The bottom floor, relatively unused, is specifically for use for the airport's luggage train.

There are separate terminal sections for certain airlines, set conveniently at 4-6 points around a square section (as seen from above).

Keep in mind that there is no effective shuttle that can take you from one terminal to another. However, if you ask, terminal staff may be able to assist in helping to hire you some help without charging you a fee in turn. Follow the signs on the arrivals level outside the building.

From the Southwest Airlines, terminal's gate side, you can see a Hyatt hotel on the level above this airport.

Food choices may differ between the different gates/terminals. Bring more money than you would spend at a traditional restaurant of the same type outside the airport or buy the items off-property before you plan to reach this airport.

Check the weather (including the forecasted temperature on the flight day). You should generally dress cooler for the warm or hot weather when arriving at this airport. Temperatures are about 10 degrees higher outside at this airport than most other airports around the United States.

Warnings

All the terminals have food choices right outside the gate areas. Don't let them lead you awry. Unless you want to double your expenses don't overspend. There are other booths inside the gate areas, but these could be problematic.

Own a Segway machine? TSA won't allow you to pass through the check-in desk as they interfere with security procedures and must be checked as regular flight baggage upon reaching the check-in desk near the entrance.

xercises

1. Vocabulary

(1) The invention would have wide (   ) in industry.

    A. apply   B. benefit   C. application   D. spread

(2) Emotional upsets (   ) powerful and deadly toxic substances.

    A. generate   B. release   C. produce   D. create

(3) We are confident of a successful (   ).

    A. increase   B. achievement   C. fruit   D. outcome

(4) Turkey plans to (   ) the waters of the Tigris and Euphrates rivers for big hydro-electric power projects.

    A. harness   B. handedness   C. harshness   D. happiness

(5) The group is working to promote the (   ) of broadband wireless access over long distances.

    A. adoption   B. usefulness   C. ceaseless   D. uselessness

2. Dialogue

(1) P: My flight will depart at Gate B25.（您能告诉我怎么去吗？）

    O: Please go straight and turn left in 100 meters. Gate B25 is at the end of the corridor.

(2) P:（我怎样找到登机口？）

    O: It will be easy to find. Each gate is clearly marked.

    P: I see. Thank you very much.

3. Translate

(1) Starting on June 30, 2018, if you are traveling from an international last-point-of-departure to the U.S., powder-based substances in carry-on baggage greater than 350ml or 12 oz.

may require additional screening at the central checkpoint.

(2) Powder-like substances over 12 oz. or 350ml in carry-on that cannot be resolved at the central checkpoint will not be allowed onto the cabin of the aircraft and will be disposed of.

(3) For your convenience, place powders in your checked bag.

(4) The measures have already been implemented at U.S. airports nationwide to identify and prevent potentially dangerous items from being brought aboard the aircraft.

(5) There are no changes to what is allowed in carry-on baggage at U.S. airport checkpoints.

ialogue

Special Circumstances

Dialogue 1

O: Excuse me, whose bag is this?

P: Oh, it's mine. Is there anything wrong?

O: Yes, something in the baggage is leaking.

P: Oh, I can smell it. It's perfume. I dropped my bag on the ground when getting out of the taxi. It must have broken.

O: It's a great pity, but you have to clean up your baggage.

P: I will take it and clean it up. I'm sorry about the smell.

O: You can clean it in the restroom.

P: Thank you.

O: My pleasure. Bye-bye.

P: Bye.

Dialogue 2

O: Is this your baggage?

P: Yes. Can I take it away now?

O: You can, but I see there is a broken bottle inside.

P: Oh my god. It's makeup that I bought for my best friend. What will I do now?

O: I'm sorry. I guess you can buy another one in the duty-free shop if you like.

P: That sounds good. Thank you very much.

O: My pleasure. Have a good journey.

Dialogue 3

O: Excuse me, sir. This way please.

O: Please show me your passport and boarding pass. Also, place your bags on the belt.

P: I'm a special envoy from the Embassy in Beijing. I think my documents and my bags are exempt from examinations.

O: Sorry. That is true for the customs check, but there is no exemption for security check even if you are a diplomat.

P: OK. Here you are.

O: Thank you for your cooperation.

The officer checks the passport and boarding pass, and returns them to the passenger.

O: You can pass through the X-ray machine and pick up your bags now. Have a good trip.

P: Thank you.

 Text

Understanding Airport Security Rules

Navigating airport security checkpoints can be a **tedious** exercise for travelers. But the process for getting on an airplane can become less **burdensome** if travelers know why certain procedures are in place.

Transportation Security Administration spokesperson J. Kawika Riley said the group's goal is to reduce risk while minimizing inconvenience to travelers at checkpoints.

"Transportation security is a balancing act." Riley said.

According to Riley, the only way to make air travel 100 percent secure is to **eliminate** air travel altogether. That's not an option for most travelers. It helps travelers to be informed about why security procedures exist. Here are the most common TSA-enforced, airline security procedures and why they exist:

Take your laptop out of its bag and put it into a separate bin.

TSA agents examine laptops for explosives "that appear benign," but that could be hidden within the body of computers and electronic equipment, Riley said. TSA can more easily, clearly and quickly examine a laptop if it is **isolated** in a bin. If you don't want to take your computer out each time, purchase a TSA-approved bag that offers a clear image of the computer in the X-ray machine.

Limit liquids, gels and aerosols to 3 ounces or less and place them all in a clear, one-quart, zip-top bag.

Many people don't understand how their toothpaste or perfume could seem dangerous. But when several, UK-based **terrorists** were caught **plotting** to blow up at least 10 airliners with ordinary-looking, small-liquid explosives 5 years ago, explosives experts re-evaluated security procedures. They determined that it is unlikely for a terrorist to assemble and ignite an explosion device from several small containers and no matches. Screening technology for checked luggage can detect an assembled bomb, but it's more difficult for checkpoint machines to detect them. Keeping some liquids together in the plastic bag makes the screening process quicker and more efficient.

Remove your hats, shoes, belts and jackets.

Small weapons and other hazardous items can be easily hidden in these items. After Richard Colvin Reid — the "Shoe Bomber" — tried **detonating** an explosive hidden in his shoes on a commercial airliner in 2001, TSA began screening loose items separately. Belts and other metal accessories cause false metal detector alarms. By removing them, the alarm will detect any other prohibited metal items on your person.

Walk through body scanners.

Metal detectors screen for such items as guns, knives and other prohibited items but Advanced Imaging Technology scanners, which were **implemented** in 2010, screen passengers for non-metallic prohibited items, such as matches or drugs. Gutheinz says the scanners are effective because a TSA screener can check underneath a passenger's clothing for hidden prohibited items. The process takes a matter of seconds **versus** a 2-to-5-minute pat down. Travelers can expect that as long as terrorism threats **evolve**, aviation security procedures will too. Get through the security line faster by being prepared. As you comply with airport security rules, remember the goal: to keep us all a little safer.

Vocabulary

tedious	['tiːdiəs]	If you describe something such as a job, task, or situation as tedious, you mean it is boring and rather frustrating. *adj.* 单调沉闷的；冗长乏味的；令人生厌的 We had to listen to the tedious details of his operation. 我们不得不听他唠叨他那次行动的琐碎细节。
burdensome	['bɜːdnsəm]	If you describe something as burdensome, you mean it is worrying or hard to deal with. *adj.* 繁重的，烦累的，难以承担的；累赘 The load was too burdensome.　工作过于繁重。
eliminate	[ɪ'lɪmɪneɪt]	To eliminate something, especially something you do not want or need, means to remove it completely. *v.* 排除，清除；淘汰；消灭 You could never eliminate risk, but preparation and training could attenuate it.　风险不可能完全消除，但可以通过防范和培训来降低。
isolated	['aɪsəleɪtɪd]	without much contact with other people or other countries *adj.* 隔离的；孤独的；单独的；偏远的 *v.* 使隔离（isolate 的过去式和过去分词）；使孤立；使绝缘；脱离 Elderly people easily become socially isolated.　上了年纪的人很容易变得与社会隔绝。
terrorists	['terərɪsts]	A terrorist is a person who uses violence, especially murder and bombing, in order to achieve political aims. *n.* 恐怖主义者，恐怖分子（terrorist 的名词复数） One American was killed and three were wounded in

terrorist attacks. 在几起恐怖袭击中，一名美国人遇
难，三人受伤。

plot [plɒt] If people plot to do something or plot something that is illegal or wrong, they plan secretly to do it.

n. 阴谋；情节；一块土地

v. 图谋；计划；设计情节；标绘出位置；绘制

Prosecutors in the trial allege the defendants plotted to overthrow the government. 检方在审判中指称被告密谋推翻政府。

detonating ['dɛtə,net] If someone detonates a device such as a bomb, or if it detonates, it explodes.

v. （使）爆炸，引爆（detonate 的现在分词）

Two other bombs failed to detonate. 另外两枚炸弹未引爆。

implemented ['ɪmplɪmentɪd] If you implement something such as a plan, you ensure that what has been planned is done.

v. 实现（implement 的过去式和过去分词）；执行；贯彻；使生效

The government promised to implement a new system to control financial loan institutions. 政府许诺实施新的制度来控制金融贷款机构。

versus ['vɜːsəs] used to compare two different ideas, choices, etc

prep. （表示两队或双方对阵）对；（比较两种不同想法、选择等）与……相对；对抗

It was the promise of better job opportunities versus the inconvenience of moving away and leaving her friends. 那是她较好的就业前景与搬走并远离朋友的不便之间的矛盾。

evolve [i'vɒlv] to develop gradually, especially from a simple to a more complicated form; to develop sth in this way

v. （使）逐渐形成/演变；进化

The idea evolved from a drawing I discovered in the attic. 这种想法是从我在阁楼里发现的一幅画得到启发的。

译文

了解机场安全规则

对旅客来说，通过机场安全检查站可能是一项乏味的事情。但是，如果旅客知道为什么采取这些检查程序，登机过程就会变得轻松一些。

运输安全管理局（TSA）发言人 J.卡维卡·莱利表示，该组织的目标是降低风险，同时最大限度地减少在检查站给旅客带来的不便。

"运输安全是一种平衡行为。"莱利说。

根据莱利的说法，使航空旅行 100%安全的唯一方法是完全消除航空旅行。大多数旅行者都不会这么选择。机场安全规则可以帮助旅行者了解为什么安检措施会存在。以下是 TSA 最常见的安检程序及其存在的原因。

将您的笔记本电脑从包中取出并放入单独的箱子里。

莱利说，TSA 检查笔记本电脑，检查这些"看似无害"的物品，因为爆炸物可能隐藏在计算机和电子设备的内部。如果笔记本电脑被放在箱子里，TSA 可以更轻松、清晰和快速地检查笔记本电脑。如果您不想每次都把笔记本电脑拿出来，请购买 TSA 批准的袋子，它可以使笔记本电脑在 X 光机中显示清晰的图像。

将液体、凝胶和气雾剂的重量限制在 3 盎司或更少，并将它们全部放入一个一夸脱的透明拉链袋中。

许多人不明白他们的牙膏或香水为什么看起来很危险。但是，当 5 年前几名英国恐怖分子被发现密谋用外观普通的小型液体炸药炸毁至少 10 架客机时，炸药专家重新评估了安检程序。他们认为，恐怖分子不太可能在没有火柴的情况下，用几个小容器组装并点燃爆炸装置。托运行李的安检技术可以检测到组装好的炸弹，但检查点的 X 光机却很难探测到炸弹。将一些液体放在塑料袋中可使检查过程更快、更有效。

脱掉帽子、鞋子、腰带和夹克。

小型武器和其他危险物品很容易隐藏在这些物品中。2001 年，"鞋子炸弹"理查德·科尔文·里德试图在一架商用客机上引爆藏在他鞋子里的炸药后，TSA 开始单独检查零散的物品。皮带和其他金属配件会导致金属探测器发出错误的警报。通过移除它们，金属探测器将检测到您身上的任何其他违禁金属物品。

步入式身体扫描仪。

金属探测器会筛查枪支、刀具和其他违禁物品等物品，但 2010 年投入使用的高级成像技术扫描仪会筛查乘客的非金属违禁物品，如火柴或毒品。古特海因次说扫描仪很有效，因为 TSA 安检员可以检查乘客衣服下面是否有隐藏违禁物品。这个过程需要几秒钟，而不是 2～5 分钟的搜身检查。旅客可以预期，魔高一尺，道高一丈，只要恐怖主义威胁

不断演变，民航安检程序也会随之演变。旅客有备而来，从而更快地通过安检通道。当
您遵守机场安全规则时，请记住这个目标：让我们所有人都更安全。

How to Secure Your Luggage for a Flight

Flying is a convenient way to get long distances, but there are plenty of potential dangers
for you and your stuff. Even with increased security in airports, plenty of items are lost and
stolen from people's luggage. In order to secure your luggage for air travel, you will want to
find ways to discourage potential thieves from breaking into your suitcase and let you know
quickly if someone has done so. You can take several steps at home, in the airport, and even on
board the plane to make sure all of your stuff arrives with you, safe and sound.

Part 1 Packing Your Bag

1

Find out what you can pack. Airlines post their restrictions online, so you should be able
to check them easily. Avoid packing inappropriate or disallowed items, as that will prevent you
from having to open your bag and remove them in the airport. This will weaken your other
security steps, making your bag more vulnerable.

2

Consider buying a hard-sided suitcase. Most common suitcases are made of fabric and open and close through zippers. A resourceful thief can easily bypass your lock by cutting through the fabric or using a pen to open the zipper. A hard case with clasps will be much more difficult to break into, and many thieves are looking for easy marks.

3

Remove batteries from any item. The last thing you want is for electronic or battery-powered items from turning on in flight or while getting checked by security. Items running can draw the attention of security, and make it more likely they search your bag, making it less secure. Remove batteries or other power devices before packing to make sure nothing goes off at an inopportune time.

4

Put labels on your luggage. Make sure you, and anyone who finds your luggage, knows it belongs to you. Your label should give your name, a destination address, and contact information like an email address and cell phone number. This way, if something happens to your bag, it will be much easier for the person who finds it to let you know where it is.

One other good travel tip is to remove tags or stickers from previous flights. This will help to prevent the airline from accidentally sending your bag elsewhere than your destination.

5

Use a lock. Close up your bag and use a lock to hold it shut. When you buy a lock for your luggage, make sure what you buy fits the case, otherwise you won't be able to close your suitcase properly. A thick shackle is better, as it will be harder to pick or cut off. If your lock opens with a key, remember to keep that key with you at all times, probably best with the rest of your valuables.

TSA-approved locks can be opened with particular keys held by TSA agents. Be warned, though, that those keys can be copied, and are not difficult to acquire online. In addition, many can be picked or broken relatively easily. You do not need to have a TSA-approved lock on your luggage, though if you don't have one, TSA will break it if they feel they need to get into your bags.

If you use multiple locks, consider mixing the type of lock you use. This will help protect against criminals who only have one way to get through a lock, and can discourage would-be thieves.

If your carry-on bag has a lock on it, be sure to use it when you board the plane. It can be a hassle to open again if you need something, but that way it is always locked if you should go to the bathroom or take a nap.

Part 2　Walking Through the Airport

1

Keep your bags with you at all times. Do your best to never let your bags out of your sight. Carry it with you everywhere you go in the airport, and watch them carefully. This will lessen the chances of someone walking off with your bag, or digging around where they shouldn't be.

In the few places that you can't hold on to your bags, like at security, do your best to keep an eye on it. Watch to make sure your bag or bin goes into the X-ray machine, and to make sure it comes back out. Once your items are through, grab them and get away from the security point. You can put on your shoes elsewhere.

2

Keep valuables in your carry-on bags. This includes items you will want or need on the plane like your wallet, boarding pass, passport, driver's license, or medicine. You want to keep valuable items near you as much as possible, which limits the chance of their being lost or stolen.

3

Put these valuables in one place. Keeping these things in one place will help you if you need to look for them, as they will all be together and easily accessible. Alternatively, if you can't find them quickly, you'll notice right away that things are missing, and can alert the proper authorities.

4

Wrap your luggage in plastic. One way to discourage potential thieves is to wrap your suitcases in saran wrap or other plastic coverings. This won't necessarily prevent someone from getting into your suitcase, as it is very easy to cut. However, it will let you know almost immediately if someone has tampered with your luggage when you retrieve it. This may cause potential thieves who are looking for stealth to skip your bag.

Some major airports have wrapping service stations. You can pay for a machine to give you the plastic to wrap the bag after arriving at the airport.

5

Decorate your bag. While you don't want to bring expensive, fancy suitcases on your flight, you should be willing to add some kind of customization to your luggage. A fun sticker, colorful ribbons, or even just a different color luggage strap should be enough to let you know which bag is yours at a glance. This will make it easier to find when you arrive, and let you know very quickly if your bag is missing. It will also make it less likely that someone will take your bag by mistake.

Part 3　Securing Your Items During the Flight

1

Board the plane early. This will guarantee you can get space in the overhead bins and won't need to check any luggage at the gate. You will also get your pick of the bins, so you can make sure your bag is close to you during the flight. Consider purchasing priority boarding privileges with your ticket, or signing up for a frequent flyer program that may give you that access in order to get on your plane quickly.

2

Bury your wallet on board. Once you get on the plane, your need for items in your wallet like cash is minimal. Take the chance to bury it in your luggage, deep in the bag, which will make it harder for someone to slip it out during the flight. If it's deep enough, someone who wanted to take it would need to take your entire bag and empty it out.

3

Store your bag near you. Some people, when travelling at the back of the plane, like to store their bags up near the front, thinking it will make it easier to get off the plane. This will separate you from your bag, and make it much harder to keep track of who may be looking into your stuff. The closer your bag is to you, the easier it will be to watch.

One good place for storing your bag is the overhead compartment across from your seat, rather than the one directly above you. This will allow you to see the compartment if someone should open it.

4

Put your bag upside down. When you load your luggage into the overhead compartment, make sure it goes in with the zippers and pockets facing inward. This will make it harder to open your bag, at least without you or someone else noticing.

Alternatively, make sure the pockets are toward you when you put the bag under the seat. You don't want the person in front of you to be able to reach down and pull something out that you can't see. If you can see the pockets, you can see who is accessing them.

5

Speak up if you see something. If you notice someone handling your luggage who shouldn't be, say something. Firmly acknowledging the potential theft should be enough to stop what is going on. If you do notice theft, stealing from luggage or stealing the luggage itself, let the flight attendant or security guard know immediately.

Warnings

Sometimes the TSA is going to break through your security steps to open and check your luggage. Remember that even if you don't like the airline's rules, you still need to follow them, and security checks will likely make your luggage less secure.

If you do get pulled out of line, or parts of your bag are searched, answer every question as completely and honestly as possible. You don't want to give security agents a reason to further root around in your luggage, as this can undermine your other security features.

Exercise

1. Vocabulary

(1) You could never (   ) risk, but preparation and training could attenuate it.

    A. eliminate   B. remove   C. increase   D. reduce

(2) Elderly people easily become socially (   ).

    A. quarantined   B. isolated   C. closed   D. separated

(3) One American was killed and three were wounded in the (   ) attacks.

    A. terror   B. terrorism   C. terrorist   D. terrifying

(4) Two other bombs failed to (   ).

    A. bomb   B. detonate   C. burst   D. blast

(5) The government promised to install a new system to (   ) control over financial loan institutions.

    A. use   B. utilize   C. enrich   D. implement

2. Dialogue

(1) O: Excuse me,（这是谁的包？）

    P: Oh, it's mine.（有什么问题吗？）

(2) O:（是的，行李里面有东西漏出来了。）

    P: Oh, I can smell it.（是香水。）（我下出租车时把包掉在地上了。一定是碎了。）

3. Translate

（1）乘客仍然把他们的随身行李通过 X 光机检查。

（2）如果 X 光线机检测到潜在危险的粉末，装粉末的容器会被拿出来，从中取一个小样本，并将样本与溶液混合进行测试。

（3）在去年年底的试点测试中，"很小一部分"的行李流需要额外的测试。

（4）绝大多数常见的粉末——婴儿配方奶粉、药物和化妆品——不需要额外的筛查。

（5）如果粉末确实需要另一个级别的筛选，它将以一种避免产品污染的方式进行，乘客将了解测试结果。

 **ialogue**

Settling Problem

Dialogue 1

One officer notices there is a bag left beside the checking table. No passenger claims it. The officers are going to take the appropriate security measure. One passenger comes to the checkpoint in a hurry.

P: Excuse me, I lost my bag.

O: Please describe your bag, such as the size, color, and so on.

P: It is a blue carry-on bag, and it has a red tag on it.

O: Yes, this is your bag.

P: Thank you very much.

O: Please do not leave your bag unattended next time. It causes a problem for security.

P: I am so sorry. Thank you very much.

O: My pleasure.

Dialogue 2

P: Excuse me, sir.

O: Can I help you?

P: I'm here to meet my friend. The flight number is CA174. Has the flight arrived at the airport?

O: I'm not sure. You can check an electronic display screen.

P: Where is the electronic display screen?

O: There are many all over the airport. The nearest one is over there.

P: OK. Thank you.

O: You are welcome.

Dialogue 3

O: Please show me your passport and boarding pass, and place your bags on the belt to be checked

P: I'm a diplomat. According to the international practices, my documents and baggage are exempt from examinations.

O: Sorry. That is true for the customs check. But there is no exemption for security check even if you are a diplomat. This is international practice.

P: I'm a special envoy of the Embassy in Beijing. I should enjoy the diplomatic immunity.

O: Sorry. Even the ambassador has to go through this check. Please cooperate with us.

P: What will happen if I refuse the check?

O: If so, you will not be allowed to pass through this security check point and you will miss your flight.

P: OK. I give in this time, but I will write a letter to your government about this.

O: Sorry. I'm just an officer. It is my duty to carry out the security check. But as a diplomat, you should know how to respect the law of other countries.

Face Scans Are Speeding up Airport Security

Who cares if you hate it? This time- and effort-saving tech is spreading, and fast.

Over the next three years, 77 percent of airports and 71 percent of airlines are planning trials or full rollouts of biometric scanning systems.

What many people call airports, you likely know as one huge **queue**. From curb to gate, zigzagging between retractable barriers, from one pinch point to the next — in industry **parlance**, this is your travel ribbon, flowing, or jamming, through the terminal. Check in, bag drop, security, the coffee shop, the lounge, the boarding gate, the halting march down the aisle.

Now imagine a future free of security gates, where you walk from the curb to your plane as easily as you unlock your phone, without needing to worry about the dangers that come with air travel in the 21st century. Such is the promise of airports taking advantage of **biometric** data, using facial recognition and other AI-powered techniques to recognize, authorize, and screen you from afar. Here, the division between the airport's monitored interior and the outside world melts away out of necessity.

"If you walk into the airport and immediately the airport authority knows who you are, you don't need such a strict division," says Max Hirsh, who researches airports and urban development at Hong Kong University. This may sound like a **utopian** vision or a privacy nightmare. Either way, it is already happening.

The components that make a free-flowing facial-recognition system work are already in real-world trials. Delta is calling its terminal at Atlanta's Hartsfield-Jackson Airport the first biometric terminal in the US. Travelers flying direct to an international **destination** enter their passport details into the app on their phone when they check in. Then they can drop their bags, walk up to the TSA checkpoint without showing their ID and boarding pass again (although screening is still conventional X-ray and body scanners, for now), and stroll through the boarding gate just by looking at a camera and waiting for a green check mark to flash on the screen.

This is just the beginning. Over the next three years, 77 percent of airports and 71 percent of airlines are planning trials or full rollouts of biometric scanning systems, according to SITA, an IT company that builds airport tech.

"This is the first time we've been able to pull together the vision that we've had for 24 months, where every step of the way through the travel ribbon, you can see that technology operating," says Gareth Joyce, who manages airport customer service for Delta.

It takes just two seconds for the computer to recognize passengers at the gate, he says, which saves nine minutes total to board a flight of 275 people. The boarding system is working so well that Delta has begun using it at New York's JFK and Detroit Metropolitan Wayne County airports.

British Airways is using facial recognition to put people on planes in Los Angeles, Orlando, Miami, and New York. Glass security barriers block the jet bridge when a passenger walks up. Then a camera slides up or down inside a slim white pillar, snaps their profile, and flashes a green check mark (or a red cross if it doesn't recognize them). And look the glass swooshes open. The airline says it can board 400 passengers in just 22 minutes, which is twice as fast as the standard method.

If the idea of having your face being scanned creeps you out, you should know there's a reason the US is pioneering this tech. The government has your image anyway. Airlines are testing these systems on international flights because the **database** of faces they rely on comes from US Customs and Border Protection.

That agency already has a record of people's faces, and often other biometrics like **fingerprints**, from passport and visa applications or from when visitors go through immigration entering the country. CBP shares access to that information with airlines for them to check against. "They tell the airline who the traveler is, so they can **automate** the boarding process, and it becomes a very simple seamless process," says Sean Farrell, who heads biometrics and passenger processing at SITA. And security is improved at the same time.

"We do not store or maintain customer images," Delta's Joyce says. The airline checks an **encrypted** photo image against the CBP database and gets a yes or no in response. He says only 2 percent of customers opt out of the facial-recognition tech when given the option to use it.

That's great, if it works reliably. Recent airline IT failures, like a system outage that grounded 650 Delta flights in 2016, have highlighted just how dependent air travel is on well-connected, smoothly functioning computer systems. So adding more tech will need to be done carefully. SITA's research also shows over a third of airlines are worried about the challenge of integrating the new tools into existing systems, and a lack of standards for doing it.

"When using airport terminals as a place to beta test them, it's inevitable there will be glitches leading to delays." Hirsh says. A cleverly designed biometric system will allow airlines to quickly switch to a paper-based backup, which, though it might be slower, will at least allow passengers to board and planes to leave. And when they work, biometrics could make that ribbon flow through the airport a little more smoothly.

Vocabulary

creepy	['kriːpi]	causing an unpleasant feeling of fear or slight horror *adj.* 令人毛骨悚然的；爬行的 It's kind of creepy down in the cellar! 地窖里真令人有点不寒而栗！
queue	[kjuː]	a line of people, cars, etc. waiting for sth or to do sth *n.*（人、汽车等的）队，行列 How long were you in the queue? 你排多长时间队了？
parlance	['paːləns]	a particular way of using words or expressing yourself, for example one used by a particular group *n.* 说法；用语；术语 The phrase is common diplomatic parlance for spying. 这种说法是对间谍行为的常用外交辞令。
biometric	[ˌbaɪəʊ'metrɪk]	using measurements of human features, such as fingers or eyes, in order to identify people *adj.* 生物统计的；生物特征识别的 Biometric passports are making matters worse. 生物识别式护照使事态变得更糟。
utopian	[juː'təʊpiən]	having a strong belief that everything can be perfect, often in a way that does not seem to be realistic or practical *adj.* 乌托邦的；空想的；理想化的 His was a utopian vision of nature in its purest form. 他对大自然的看法是一种最纯粹的乌托邦式看法。
destination	[ˌdestɪ'neɪʃn]	a place to which sb/sth is going or being sent *n.* 目的地，终点 Our luggage was checked all the way through to our final destination. 我们的行李一直被托运到最

		终目的地。
database	['deɪtəbeɪs]	an organized set of data that is stored in a computer and can be looked at and used in various ways *n.* 数据库，资料库 The state maintains a database of names of people allowed to vote. 该州有一个可以投票的人的姓名数据库。
fingerprint	['fɪŋgəprɪnt]	a mark made by the pattern of lines on the tip of a person's finger, often used by the police to identify criminals *n.* 指纹；手印 The detective discovered no fewer than 35 fingerprints. 这名侦探发现了不下 35 个指纹。
automate	['ɔːtəmeɪt]	to use machines and computers instead of people to do a job or task *vt.* 使自动化，使自动操作 He wanted to use computers to automate the process. 他想用电脑来使流程自动化。
encrypt	[ɪn'krɪpt]	to put information into a special code, especially in order to prevent people from looking at it without authority *v.* 把……加密，将……译成密码 The system lets you encrypt or scramble the data that's sent between machines. 这个系统可以让你对机器间互发的数据作加密或扰频处理。

译文

加快机场安检速度的面部扫描技术正在迅速普及

谁在乎你是否讨厌它？这种省时省力的技术正在迅速传播。

在接下来的三年里，77% 的机场和 71% 的航空公司正在计划试验或全面推出生物识别扫描系统。

很多人所说的机场，你可能知道意味着排长队。从控点到登机口，在可伸缩屏障之间蜿蜒前进，从一个控点到下一个控点——用行业术语来说，这就是你的旅行带，流动的，或拥挤的，整个候机楼都是这样。登机、行李托运、安检、咖啡厅、休息室、登机口，以及在通道上的蹒跚行走。

现在想象一下没有安检门的未来，您可以像解锁手机一样轻松地从隔离区登上飞机，而无须担心 21 世纪航空旅行带来的危险。这就是机场利用生物识别数据、使用面部识别和其他人工智能技术从远处识别、授权和扫描的承诺。在这里，机场内部监控区域和外部世界之间的界限因为没有必要而消失了。

"如果你走进机场，机场方面立即知道你是谁，你就不需要这么严格的划分了。"香港大学研究机场和城市发展的马克斯·赫什说。这听起来像是乌托邦式的愿景，也可能是隐私噩梦。不管怎样，这一切已经发生了。

旅客可自由走动的面部识别工作系统构件，已经在现实世界中进行了试验。达美航空将其位于亚特兰大哈兹菲尔德−杰克逊机场的候机楼称为美国第一个生物识别候机楼。直接飞往国际目的地的旅客，在办理登机手续时，在手机上的应用程序中输入他们的护照详细信息。然后他们可以放下行李，走到 TSA 检查站，而无须再次出示身份证件和登机牌（尽管目前的检查仍然是传统的 X 射线和身体扫描仪），然后只需看着镜头并等待绿色对勾在屏幕上闪烁，即可漫步通过登机口。

这仅仅是个开始。据一个称为 SITA 的搭建机场人工智能技术的 IT 公司说，在接下来的三年里，77%的机场和 71%的航空公司正在计划试验或全面推出生物识别扫描系统。

"这是我们第一次能够将 24 个月来的愿景整合在一起，通过旅行带的每一步，您都可以看到该技术正在运行。"达美航空的机场客户服务经理加雷斯乔伊斯说。

他说，计算机只需两秒钟就可以识别出登机口的乘客，这使载客 275 人的航班登机时间总共节省了 9 分钟。登机系统运行良好，达美航空已开始在纽约肯尼迪机场和底特律大都会韦恩县机场使用它。

英国航空公司正在使用面部识别技术让乘客搭乘洛杉矶、奥兰多、迈阿密和纽约的飞机。当乘客走上飞机时，玻璃安检屏障会挡住登机桥。然后一个相机在细长的白色柱子内上下滑动，捕捉他们的轮廓，并闪烁一个绿色的对勾标记（如果无法识别，则显示一个红十字）。瞧，玻璃门迅速打开了。该航空公司表示，它可以在短短 22 分钟内，让400 名乘客登机，这是标准方法的两倍。

如果你的脸被扫描的让你觉得恐惧，你应该知道美国开创这项技术是有原因的。不管怎样，政府有你的图像。航空公司正在国际航班上测试这些系统，因为他们依赖的人脸数据库来自美国海关和边境保护局。

该机构已经从护照和签证申请中或在游客通过移民局进入该国时获得了人脸记录，通常还有指纹等其他生物识别信息。CBP 与航空公司共享对这些信息的访问权限，以便航空公司进行核对。"它们告诉航空公司旅客是谁，这样航空公司就可以自动化登机流程，这将成为一个非常简单的无缝流程。" SITA 的生物识别和旅客信息处理负责人肖恩·法雷尔说。同时也提高了安全性。

"我们不存储或维护客户图像，"达美航空的乔伊斯说。航空公司根据 CBP 数据库检查加密的照片图像，并得到是或否的回应。他说，只有2%的客户在选择使用面部识别技术时会选择退出。

如果它运行可靠的话那就太好了。最近的航空公司 IT 故障，如 2016 年导致的 650架达美公司航班停飞的系统中断，凸显了航空旅行对连接良好和运行顺畅的计算机系统的依赖程度。因此，使用更多的新技术，需要谨慎。SITA 的研究还显示，超过三分之一的航空公司担心将新技术集成到现有系统中的风险，而且也缺乏相关标准。

"当使用机场航站楼作为对它们进行 Beta 测试的地方时，不可避免地会出现导致延误的故障。"赫什说。一个设计巧妙的生物识别系统将使航空公司能够快速切换到纸质备份，虽然它可能会更慢，但至少可以让乘客登机和飞机离开。当它们工作时，生物识别技术可以让拥挤的旅客流更顺畅地流过机场。

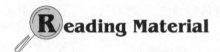

How to Find Your TSA Precheck Number

In the US, the Transportation Security Administration (TSA) offers 4 programs that get you access to the TSA Precheck lines. If you're enrolled in Precheck, you don't have to remove your shoes, belt, or light jacket. You also don't have to take laptops out of their cases. This makes getting on an airplane a lot less of a hassle. Once you're enrolled, simply enter your known traveler number (KTN), also called a TSA travel number or a TSA number, when you make your airline reservations. If you've forgotten your TSA Precheck number, the easiest way to retrieve it is from the website for the TSA's Trusted Traveler Program.

Method 1　Locating Your KTN

1

Look for your membership card. If you enrolled in the Global Entry, NEXUS, or SENTRI programs, the PASSID printed on the back of your card also serves as your KTN. If you previously enrolled in the Precheck program and then enrolled in Global Entry, NEXUS, or SENTRI, use the PASSID instead.

Your PASSID is a 9-digit number that usually starts with 15, 98, or 99.

Because the Global Entry, NEXUS, or SENTRI programs provide additional services not available with the TSA Precheck program, your enrollment in these programs supersedes your enrollment in Precheck.

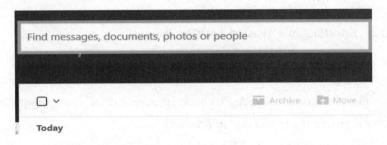

2

Check your approval letter if you enrolled in the Precheck program. The TSA sends a written notification when your enrollment in the Precheck program is approved. This letter has your KTN on it.

Search your personal records to see if you saved this letter. If you did, you can find your TSA Precheck number that way.

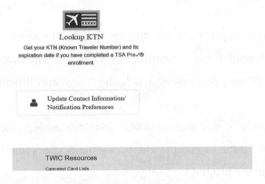

3

Go to the Trusted Traveler Program website if you can't find your card. Go to https://universalenroll.dhs.gov/programs/precheck and scroll down to the bottom of the page. Click the blue icon with the words "Lookup KTN."

Provide the information requested exactly as you submitted it when you enrolled in the program.

If you can't recall your UE ID, call 855-DHS-UES1 (855-347-8371). Customer service staff are available to assist you Monday through Friday from 8 a.m. to 10 p.m. Eastern time.

Tip: If you enrolled in Global Entry, NEXUS, or SENTRI, use the service at https://secure.login.gov/ instead.

Method 2   Enrolling in a Trusted Traveler Program

1

Choose the program that best meets your needs. The TSA offers 4 Trusted Traveler programs that include access to TSA Precheck lines. Some of these programs also offer expedited customs processing in addition to Precheck access.

TSA Precheck enables access to TSA Precheck lines for departures from all US airports. US citizens and lawful permanent residents are eligible.

Global Entry enables access to TSA Precheck lines as well as expedited entry to the US from international destinations. US citizens, lawful permanent residents, and select foreign nationals are eligible.

NEXUS enables access to TSA Precheck lines as well as expedited entry to the US from Canada. US citizens, lawful permanent residents, Canadian citizens, Canadian permanent residents, and Mexican nationalists are eligible.

SENTRI enables access to TSA Precheck lines as well as expedited entry to the US from Canada and Mexico. US citizens, lawful permanent residents, and all foreign nationals are potentially eligible.

2

Complete the online application. If you've decided to enroll in the TSA Precheck program, go to the Universal Enroll website at https://universalenroll.dhs.gov/. For all other programs, go to https://secure.login.gov/. Click the "new enrollment" button to start your application.

The application requires information about your citizenship, identity, and background. This information will be used to complete a background check that will indicate if you're suitable for enrollment in the program.

You can also apply in person at an enrollment center near you. To find the nearest enrollment center, go to https://universalenroll.dhs.gov/locator and enter your ZIP code, then click search.

Tip: On your application, you must provide all names or aliases you've used previously. This is necessary so the TSA can complete a thorough background check.

3

Schedule your in-person appointment. After you complete your application, you can schedule an appointment at the nearest enrollment center on the same website. The in-person appointment takes approximately 10 minutes and includes a background check and fingerprinting.

If you need to reschedule your appointment, you can do so from the same website. Many TSA Precheck enrollment centers also take walk-ins, although you may have to wait.

4

Gather documents for your appointment. The TSA has 2 lists of documents. If you have one of the documents in List A, you don't have to bring anything else. If you don't have one of the documents in List A, you'll need to bring two documents from List B.

List A documents include: unexpired passport book or card, permanent resident card, unexpired US enhanced driver's license or enhanced state-issued identity card

List B documents include: unexpired driver's license or state ID, unexpired US military ID, expired US passport within 12 months of expiration, US birth certificate, US certificate of naturalization

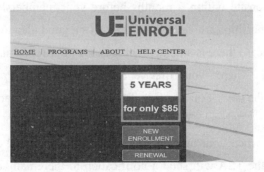

5

Attend your scheduled appointment. On the date of your appointment, take your documents to the enrollment center. It's a good idea to arrive a few minutes early. An officer will review your information and verify your documents. Then you will be fingerprinted.

You will also be photographed. The photograph is used to verify your identity at TSA checkpoints that have facial recognition technology.

6

Pay your application fee. You can pay your application fee with a major credit or debit card, personal check, certified check, or money order. As of 2019, the enrollment fee for the TSA Precheck program is $85.

If you applied for Global Entry, you must pay a one-time fee of $100 (as of 2019) online using an electronic bank transfer or a major credit or debit card. You'll pay the regular membership fee at your appointment.

OR

Enter Your Service Code   Go!

📍 Find an Enrollment Center   👤 Update Contact Information/ Notification Preferences

Related Links	TWIC Resources
Freedom of Information Act	Canceled Card Lists
Transportation Security Administration (TSA)	TWIC Qualified Reader List

7

Wait to receive written notification. Typically, you'll get your acceptance letter in the mail within 2 to 3 weeks after your in-person appointment. However, many applications are approved within a couple of days. You can check the status of your application online.

If you check your status online and it shows that your application was approved, you'll be able to get your KTN immediately. Write it down and keep it in a safe place.

Your known traveler number will also be included in your written notification. Keep the letter in a safe place so you'll have it if you ever need to find your TSA KTN.

Method 3   Renewing Your Membership

1

Go to the TSA website within 6 months before your membership expires. All Trusted Traveler program memberships are valid for 5 years. It's a good idea to renew well before your membership expires in case there is a delay in processing your renewal.

Use the website where you first enrolled. For TSA Precheck members, use https://universalenroll.dhs.gov/. For all other Trusted Traveler programs, go to https://secure. login.gov/.

If you're not sure when your membership expires, you can find out by logging onto the website. Additionally, the TSA will send a notification to the email address on file when it's time for you to renew.

Tip: You must renew within one year of the date of expiration if you want to keep the same KTN. Otherwise, you'll have to go through the entire process again as a new applicant.

2

Complete the renewal application. The renewal application requires you to provide your name, date of birth, and KTN. Based on this information, your background check will be updated.

If you violate any TSA regulations or are involved in any sort of security-related incident on an airplane or at an airport, you may not be eligible to renew your enrollment.

You may be prompted to go to an enrollment center to renew your application in person. This typically happens if you changed your name or if your enrollment fingerprints were low-quality.

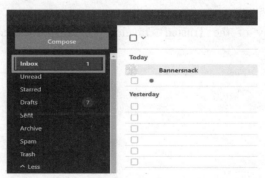

3

Pay your renewal fees online. Your renewal fee is the same as the enrollment fee. However, it's possible that the fees will increase in the 5 years since you first enrolled. You can pay with an electronic bank transfer or with a major credit or debit card.

If you applied for Global Entry, you do not have to pay the additional $100 fee again. That is a one-time enrollment fee designed to cover the costs of the background check and initial application processing.

4

Wait for notification of your renewal. The TSA will send you a written notification when your renewal has been processed. However, renewals are often processed within 2 or 3 days, so you'll know faster if you check your status online.

If you make airline reservations to fly after your membership expires, you must renew your membership before the date of your flight. Otherwise, you will not have access to TSA Precheck lines.

Contact your airline if you need to update your reservation information after renewing your membership. Renewal confirmation notifications will not allow you to access TSA Precheck lines.

Tips

Children 12 and under traveling with you can use the TSA Precheck lines without a separate membership provided you have the TSA Precheck indicator on your boarding pass.

If you forget your KTN number and have already made your airline reservation, contact the airline when you recover your number to have it added to your reservation.

If you fly with the same airline frequently, you may be able to save your KTN number with your customer profile information on the airline's website so you'll always have it available.

Warnings

The information on your Trusted Traveler membership must match the information on your ID and airline reservation, otherwise you will not be authorized to use the TSA Precheck lines.

If you enroll in the Global Entry, NEXUS, or SENTRI program, you'll receive a membership card. However, you cannot use that card to access TSA Precheck lines. You must enter your KTN when you make your airline reservation so your boarding pass is encoded with Precheck authorization.

Enrollment in any of the Trusted Traveler programs does not guarantee expedited screening.

Exercises

1. Vocabulary

(1) How long were you in the (   )?

    A. line   B. array   C. combination   D. squeue

(2) (   ) passports are making matters worse.

    A. Physical   B. Chemical   C. Biometric   D. Physiological

(3) The state maintains a (   ) of names of people allowed to vote.

    A. arsenal   B. talent pool   C. resource pool   D. resources

(4) Our luggage was checked all the way through to our final (   ).

    A. place of departure   B. memorial site

    C. encounter place   D. destination

(5) The system lets you (   ) or scramble the data that's sent between machines.

    A. decode   B. encrypt   C. code   D. disturbance

2. Dialogue

(1) P: Excuse me, I lost my bag.

    O:（请描述一下你的包，比如大小颜色样子等。）

    P: It is a blue carry-on bag and it has a red tag on it.

(2) P: I'm here to meet my friend. The flight number is CA174.（这个航班到了吗？）

    O: I'm not sure.（你可以看一下电子显示屏。）

3. Translate

(1) Any powder determined to be a potential threat will not be permitted into the secure area.

(2) In the past, transportation security officers had to rely on TSA explosive specialists or local law enforcement to check out powders that required additional screening.

(3) The kits cost an average of $145 each, the TSA said.

(4) Three years ago, the TSA and its counterparts overseas imposed severe restrictions on the amount of liquids passengers could carry on planes after British authorities uncovered a plot to use flammable liquids to destroy at least seven transatlantic airliners.

(5) Those restrictions remain in place.

 ialogue

Supervising and Guarding the Aircraft

Dialogue 1

O: Excuse me, may I have a look at your pass?

P: Oh, here you are.

O: Are you a pilot?

P: Yes, I am.

O: Which airline are you working for?

P: Air China.

O: You may go now. Thank you for your cooperation.

P: Thank you.

Dialogue 2

O: Excuse me, may I have a look at your pass?

P: Oh, sorry, I don't have it with me. I've left it in my office. I'm the technician of Southern Airlines.

O: Please go back to your office and get your pass. As the rule says, all people must have the special pass for the airport, or they cannot access this area.

P: Sorry, I was in a hurry. I will go back to my office.

O: Thanks for your cooperation.

Dialogue 3

O: Sorry, what are you doing?

P: I must go back to the airplane, I left my bag in the cabin.

O: Well, please wait for a few minutes, when all passengers have disembarked, you may return.

P: Thank you very much.

PNNL Technology

If you have been through airport security lately, you likely have done what those of us at the Department of Energy's Pacific Northwest National Laboratory call the "PNNL salute."

Airline passengers strike this pose, pausing momentarily with arms above their heads, so a PNNL-developed technology can quickly scan them for **concealed** weapons and other threats that traditional metal detectors would miss.

Scientists and engineers determined how to use non-harmful, ultrahigh-frequency radio waves — called millimeter waves — to penetrate clothing and scan for concealed objects such as liquids, gels, plastics, powders and **ceramics**.

With support from the Department of Homeland Security's Screening at Speed program, PNNL researchers continue to advance and expand **millimeter** wave technology to develop solutions for the future.

For example, they are working on a shoe scanner that could replace the **inconvenient** pre-boarding **ritual** of removing your shoes.

Integrated into existing body imaging portals, the system could provide a three-**dimensional** image of passengers' footwear while it remains on their feet — quickly identifying concealed threats.

PNNL researchers also are exploring a walk-by screening system that would one day **eliminate** the need for the PNNL salute.

The concept is akin to the futuristic technology in "Total Recall," where security officers spot a gun on Arnold Schwarzenegger's character as he walks through a subway station.

Similarly, PNNL's technology would allow passengers to walk through security checkpoints without pausing as the imaging system screened them in real time with increased efficiency and effectiveness.

Beyond passenger screening technologies, PNNL researchers are developing an ultrasensitive technology that can quickly and accurately detect vapors from explosives, deadly chemicals and **illicit** drugs.

The technology relies on a mass spectrometer, a scientific instrument that measures or detects **isotopes** and molecules of interest by separating them according to charge and mass.

As the vapor samples make their way to the spectrometer, they collide with electrically charged ions. PNNL scientists determined they could tweak these ions to selectively detect common explosive compounds or "sniff out" traces of specific narcotics and other chemicals.

With early results demonstrating greater accuracy, the technology could offer an attractive alternative to today's time-consuming methods that rely on swabs and swipes, or drug- and explosive-sniffing dogs that require expensive care and training.

PNNL researchers are working to make the technology more portable and easier to integrate with existing screening methods for use in places like airports and mail facilities.

Lastly, PNNL will soon deploy its Airport Risk Assessment Model, or ARAM, in a partnership with the Transportation Security Administration and the Seattle-Tacoma International Airport. This web-based software helps airports prioritize their resources based on risk.

With a simple click of a button, ARAM analyzes multiple sources and quantifies the core components of risk: consequences, vulnerabilities and threat magnitudes.

It then evaluates a mathematical formula that assesses the effectiveness of each security measure and determines where each resource should be deployed to maximize the potential to reduce risk.

Many of us recall the airline slogan, "flying the friendly skies," from years ago. Today, PNNL's science and technology are making it possible to detect threats, increase security and minimize risk — so we can all fly the safer skies.

Vocabulary

conceal	[kən'si:l]	to hide sb/sth *vt.* 隐藏；隐瞒 The paintings were concealed beneath a thick layer of plaster. 那些画被隐藏在厚厚的灰泥层下面。
ceramics	[sə'ræmɪks]	the art and techniques of producing articles of clay, porcelain, etc *n.* 陶瓷工艺；陶瓷制品 Silk, jade, ceramics and iron went west to Rome. 丝绸、玉器、陶瓷和铁被西传至罗马。
millimeter	['mɪlimi:tə(r)]	A millimetre is a metric unit of length that is equal to a tenth of a centimetre or a thousandth of a metre. *n.* 毫米；千分之一米 The creature is a tiny centipede, just 10 millimetres long. 那个生物是一只很小的蜈蚣，只有10毫米长。
inconvenient	[ˌɪnkən'vi:niənt]	causing trouble or problems, especially concerning what you need or would like yourself *adj.* 不方便的；引起麻烦的；造成困难的；打扰的 Can you come at 10:30? I know it's inconvenient, but I have to see you. 你能10:30来吗？我知道这不方便，但是我必须要见你。
ritual	['rɪtʃuəl]	a series of actions that are always performed in the same way, especially as part of a religious ceremony *n.* 程序；仪规；礼节；（尤指）宗教仪式；惯例；礼制 This is the most ancient, and holiest of the Shinto rituals. 这是最古老、最神圣的神道教仪式。
integrate	['ɪntɪgreɪt]	to combine two or more things so that they work together; to combine with sth else in this way *vt.* （使）合并，使……完整；使……成整体 These programs will integrate with your existing

		software. 这些程序将和你的已有软件可综合成整体。
dimension	[daɪ'menʃn]	a measurement in space, for example the height, width or length of sth *n.* 方面；[数]维；尺寸
dimensional		*adj.* 空间的；尺寸的 You will open a new dimension to your life. 你将为你的生活打开一个新的维度。
eliminate	[ɪ'lɪmɪneɪt]	to remove or get rid of sth/sb *vt.* 消除；排除 Recent measures have not eliminated discrimination in employment. 最近的举措还未能根除就业歧视。
illicit	[ɪ'lɪsɪt]	not allowed by the law *adj.* 违法的；不正当的 Various agencies gang up to combat the use of illicit drugs. 各个机构联合起来对抗非法药品的使用。
isotope	['aɪsətəʊp]	Isotopes are atoms that have the same number of protons and electrons but different numbers of neutrons and therefore have different physical properties. *n.* 同位素 复数 isotopes As an indicator of shifts in the Earth's climate, the isotope record has two advantages. 作为地球气候变化的指标，同位素记录有两个优势。

译文

PNNL 技术

如果您最近通过了机场安检，您很可能已经做了我们这些在能源部太平洋西北国家实验室的人所说的"PNNL 敬礼"。

航空公司的乘客摆出这个姿势，将手臂举过头顶暂时停顿一下，因此 PNNL 开发的技术可以快速扫描他们，寻找传统金属探测器无法发现的隐藏武器和其他威胁。

科学家和工程师决定了如何使用无害的超高频无线电波（称为毫米波）穿透衣服并

扫描隐藏的物体，如液体、凝胶、塑料、粉末和陶瓷。

在国土安全部"快速筛查"项目的支持下，PNNL 研究人员继续推进和扩展毫米波技术，以开发面向未来的解决方案。

例如，他们正在研究一种鞋子扫描仪，它可以取代不方便的脱鞋检查的登机程序。

该系统集成到现有的身体成像门户中，可以提供乘客脚下鞋子的 3D 图像——快速识别隐藏的威胁。

PNNL 研究人员还在探索一种步行筛查系统，有朝一日将消除对 PNNL 敬礼的需要。

这个概念类似于《全面召回》中的未来技术，当阿诺德·施瓦辛格扮演的角色穿过地铁站时，安保人员发现他身上有一把枪。

同样，PNNL 的技术将允许乘客走进安检点而无须暂停，因为成像系统会快速且高效地对他们进行实时检查。

除了旅客检查技术，PNNL 研究人员正在开发一种超灵敏技术，可以快速准确地检测来自爆炸物、致命化学品和非法药物的气体。

这项技术依赖于质谱仪，这是一种根据电荷和质量将同位素和分子分离，来测量或检测同位素和分子的科学仪器。

当气体样品进入质谱仪时，它们会与带电离子发生碰撞。PNNL 科学家确定他们可以调整这些离子以选择性地检测常见的爆炸性化合物，或"嗅出"特定麻醉品和其他化学物质的踪迹。

随着早期结果显示了更高的准确性，该技术可以提供更有吸引力的方法取代目前的依赖于棉签和拭子的耗时方法，或需要昂贵护理和培训费用的毒品和爆炸物嗅探犬。

PNNL 研究人员正在努力使该技术更便携，更容易与机场和邮局等场所使用的现有检查方法集成。

最后，PNNL 将很快与运输安全管理局和西雅图-塔科马国际机场合作，部署其机场风险评估模型，简称为 ARAM。这种基于网络的软件，帮助机场根据风险对其资源进行优先排序。

只需单击一个按钮，ARAM 即可分析多个风险来源，并量化风险的核心组成部分：后果、漏洞和威胁程度。

它会使用数学公式评估每个安全措施的有效性，并确定应将每个资源部署到何处，以最大限度地降低风险。

我们中的许多人都记得多年前航空公司的口号，"飞向友好的天空"。今天，PNNL 的科学和技术使检测威胁、提高安全性和最小化风险成为可能——这样我们都可以在更安全的天空中飞行。

Reading Material

How to Identify a Boeing from an Airbus

Boeing and Airbus are the two largest aircraft manufacturers. Their aircraft, used worldwide, is the backbone of the aviation industry. However, if you ever come across an airplane at the airport, you might have some trouble identifying if it's an Airbus or a Boeing. In this article, you will learn some easy techniques to tell them apart.

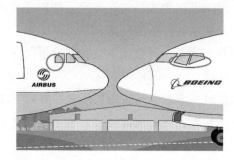

1

Look at the cockpit windows. The cockpit windows are easy ways to identify whether an aircraft is a Boeing or an Airbus. Take a look at the side of the windows, especially the angle of the last window pane.

Check to see if the side point of the conjoining of the last two window panes are angular. If the conjoining angles of the two side windows are wide and less square, it is probably a Boeing.

Check if the side of the last window pane has a sharp angle. If the window pane has a right angle (90°) or is close to a right angle at its intersection with the body of the aircraft, it's probably an Airbus.

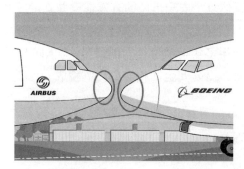

2

Look at the nose of the airplane. The nose, or the tip of the airplane, is another good sign to see if an airplane is Boeing or Airbus.

Check to see if the nose of the airplane is sharp and not round. Boeings have sharper and more pointy noses compared to an Airbus. So if the nose of the aircraft is sharp, it's probably a Boeing.

Check to see if the nose of the airplane is round. If the nose is round and resembles a semi-circle, it is probably an Airbus.

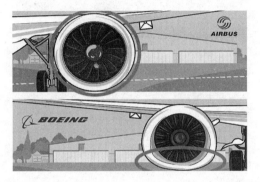

3

Look at the engines. Engines of Boeing and Airbus greatly differ from each other. Their size and shape are very different and is a telltale sign to identify whether a plane is Boeing or Airbus.

Check to see if the engines have a flat bottom. Boeing engines tend to have a very flat bottom and a more circular top.

Check to see if the engines are circular all the way. Airbus engines have a very circular engine, almost a perfect circle.

Exception: there is an exception to this, as the Boeing 777, 767, and 787 have round engines, similar to one of an Airbus.

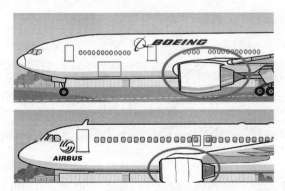

4

Look at the placement of the engines on their aircraft. Boeing and Airbus engines are placed differently.

Check to see if the engines are mounted forward. A Boeing's engine is placed at the front of the wing, not in the middle or under.

Check to see if the engines are mounted under the wing. An Airbus's engine is placed fully under the wing, so the engine is more visible if you sit closer to the rear of the plane.

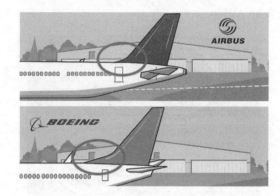

5

Look if the tail, or the fin at the back of the plane, has a slope when it reaches the plane's body.

Check to see if the tail of the plane reaches the plane's body with an extended slope. If the tail of the plane reaches the plane with an extension, causing the tail to connect with the plane less sharply, it is probably a Boeing.

Check to see if the tail of the plane connects with the plane sharply. This means that the tail reaches the plane's body with no extended slop. If it doesn't have a slope, it is an Airbus.

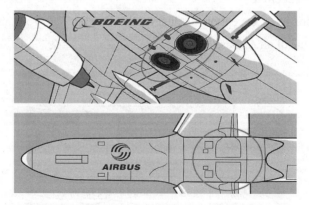

6

Look at the back gear retraction of the airplane. This is difficult to examine since this only works when a plane is taking off.

Check to see if the back gears do not have a compartment and are visible from under the plane. Boeing back gears retract into the plane, but are not covered up.

Check to see if the back gears retract into a compartment. An Airbus's gear retracts into the plane and is soon covered up, so the gear is not visible after they retract.

Method 2　Looking at Other Aspects

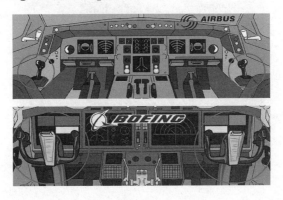

1

Take a look at the cockpit, if possible. Although this might not be permitted, it is, sometimes, possible to take a look at the cockpit.

Check to see if the airplane has a control column, also known as a yoke. A yoke is similar to a "U" shaped steering wheel, located at the front-center of both seats in the cockpit.

Check to see if a plane has a control column. If the plane doesn't have a control column, it is most likely an Airbus. Take a look at the right side of the right seat (or the left side of the left seat) to see if there is a sidestick. A sidestick looks very similar to a joystick.

Exception: while almost all Airbuses have sidesticks, the Airbus A220 has a yoke.

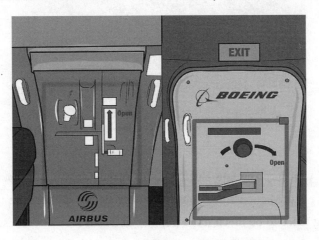

Look at the design of the emergency exits. There is a major difference between the way Boeing's emergency exits are designed and an Airbus's design.

Check the handle of the emergency exit if the airplane's emergency exits have a big spinning latch, it is probably a Boeing.

Check the handle of the emergency exit. If the plane's emergency exits don't have a big handle, but a vertical push handle, it is probably an Airbus.

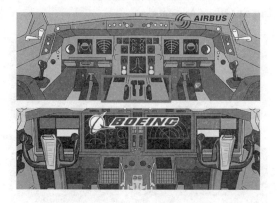

2

Take a look at the space inside of the cockpit, if possible. Boeing and Airbus cockpits differ in their size.

Examine the space between the Captain's and First Officer's seat. A Boeing tends to have less space between the two seats as well as the overall space in the cockpit.

Examine the space between the captain's and first officer's seat. An Airbus has a greater amount of space between the seats, and their cockpits are more spacious than a Boeing's.

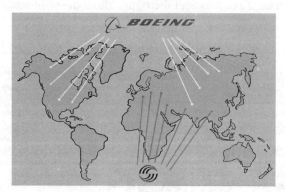

3

Estimating if your airplane is a Boeing or an Airbus depends on your location. This is only a way to make a prediction since your location does not say for sure the type of aircraft you are on. Boeing tends to be much more popular in North America and some parts of Asia, while Airbus tends to be more popular in Europe and some parts of Asia.

Warning! This can be an inaccurate way and should not be fully depended on. It is only for reference.

Tips

Examine the safety instructions card in your seat pocket. Usually, it will mention the model you are on.

Ask a crew member if you have any questions.

xercises

1. Vocabulary

(1) The paintings were (   ) beneath a thick layer of plaster.

    A. covered   B. concealed   C. cleaned   D. queue

(2) Can you come at 10:30? I know it's (   ), but I have to see you.

    A. inconvenient   B. unhappy   C. uncomfortable D. nonfluency

(3) These programs will (   ) with your existing software.

    A. merge   B. combine   C. associate   D. integrate

(4) You will open a new (   ) to your life.

    A. longitude   B. altitude   C. dimension   D. density

(5) Recent measures have not (   ) discrimination in employment.

    A. increased   B. removed   C. eliminated   D. expelled

2. Dialogue

(1) O:（你是飞行员吗？）

    P: Yes, I am.

    O:（你是哪个航空公司的？）

    P: Air China.

(2) P:（我必须回到飞机上，我的包落在机舱里了。）

    O: Well, please wait for a few minutes,（等所有旅客都下飞机了，你就可以上去了。）

3. Translate

(1) The airport launched FR-based Security Check, Intelligent Security Check Channel, and Easy Security Check platforms in 2019 and these implement full-process self-service check, further improving the passenger experience.

(2) Security is the lifeline of civil aviation, as well as an important focus of Shenzhen Airport's

smart airport construction.

(3) Shenzhen Airport uses the smart airport Security Operations Center (SOC) to build a comprehensive security support system, which provides security protection from ground to air and produces a technology-intensive, active system.

(4) The system can accurately identify potential risks, efficiently handle exceptions, and globally control airport security status.

(5) It intelligently upgrades passive airport security management to active, accurate security risk identification, prevention, and control.

 **D** ialogue

Waiting For Security Control

Dialogue 1

P: Excuse me, I have just checked in for Flight CA 879. What should I do now?

O: You should go through the passport control and security check.

P: How should we go through the security check?

O: Just put your carry-on baggage on the belt, which will take it to be screened by X-ray equipment. And you should go through that gate, the staff may give you a personal search.

Dialogue 2

P: How long will the search take?

O: It depends. If you don't have any forbidden articles, it will be very quick.

P: What kind of things can not be taken on the plane?

O: It's forbidden to carry any kind of weapons, ammunitions, aggressive tools and inflammable, explosive, corrosive, radioactive, poisonous articles on the plane.

P: Thank you.

O: You are welcome.

Dialogue 3

P: Excuse me, what's the security check for?

O: The security check is carried out for the passenger's own safety. It's for prevention of hijacking and terrorism.

P: Does everyone have to receive a personal search?

O: Yes. The personal search is made on all passengers both domestic and international.

P: What will happen to me if I refuse the security check?

O: Anyone who refuses that will not be allowed to board the flight.

Text

Fly Through Security with New Screening Technology

Security screening at Miami International Airport in the post-COVID-19 era just got easier, thanks to the installation of seven state-of-the-art computed tomography (CT) scanners at six Transportation Security Administration (TSA) checkpoints. Passengers traveling through a **lane** with a CT scanner will now be permitted to leave laptops and other electronic devices in their carry-on bags.

The new technology provides improved **explosive detection** screening by creating a 3D image that can be viewed and **rotated** on three axes for thorough visual image analysis by a TSA officer. If a bag requires further screening, TSA officers will **inspect** it to ensure that a threat item is not contained inside.

"These new scanners from the TSA are helping us streamline and **expedite** the screening process for our passengers, at a time in air travel when a smooth flowing checkpoint has never been more important. We are proud to be among the first U.S. airports to receive this **expansion** of CT technology by the TSA." says Lester Sola, MIA Director and CEO.

Like the existing CT technology used for checked baggage, the machines use **sophisticated algorithms** to detect explosives, including liquid explosives. The CT checkpoint units were designed with a smaller footprint than those used for checked baggage to allow accommodation in the constrained space of a passenger screening area. "

"TSA is focused on testing, procuring, and **deploying** additional CT systems in airports as soon as possible. TSA is continuing to develop enhanced algorithms to address evolving aviation threats while decreasing the number of physical bag searches needed to resolve alarms and thereby improve operational efficiency and automated detection. These seven units join three others previously installed when MIA became one of the first airports in the country to begin rolling out this technology in TSA checkpoints." says The Miami International Airport.

Vocabulary

lane	[leɪn]	A lane is a part of a main road which is marked by the edge of the road and a painted line, or by two painted lines. *n.* 小巷；[航][水运] 航线；车道 She signalled and pulled over into the slow lane. 她给信号后把车开进了慢车道。
explosive	[ɪk'spləʊsɪv]	a substance that is able or likely to cause an explosion *adj.* 爆炸的；爆炸性的；爆发性的 *n.* 炸药；爆炸物 The bomb was packed with several pounds of high explosive. 这枚炸弹装有几磅烈性炸药。
detection	[dɪ'tekʃn]	the process of *detecting* sth; the fact of being detected *n.* 侦查，探测；发觉，发现；察觉 Early detection of cancers is vitally important. 癌症的早期查出是极为重要的。
rotate	[rəʊ'teɪt]	to move or turn around a central fixed point; to make sth do this *n.* (使) 旋转，转动 The earth rotates around the sun. 地球围绕太阳旋转。
inspect	[ɪn'spekt]	to look closely at sth/sb, especially to check that everything is as it should be

		vt. 检查；视察；检阅；查看；审视
		Make sure you inspect the goods before signing for them. 要确保在签收货物之前进行检验。
expedite	['ekspədaɪt]	to make a process happen more quickly
		vt. 加快；促进
		We have developed rapid order processing to expedite deliveries to customers. 我们已创造了快速处理订单的方法以便迅速将货物送达顾客。
expansion	[ɪk'spænʃn]	an act of increasing or making sth increase in size, amount or importance
		n. 扩张；扩展；扩大；膨胀；阐述；扩张物
		Despite the recession the company is confident of further expansion. 尽管经济衰退，公司对进一步扩展仍充满信心。
sophisticated	[sə'fɪstɪkeɪtɪd]	clever and complicated in the way that it works or is presented
		adj. 复杂的；精致的
		Medical techniques are becoming more sophisticated all the time. 医疗技术日益复杂精妙。
algorithm	['ælgərɪðəm]	a set of rules that must be followed when solving a particular problem
		n. 算法，运算法则
		复数 algorithms
		Don't diddle code to make it faster — find a better algorithm. 不要为了使代码更快而胡乱编写代码——要找到更好的算法。
deploy	[dɪ'plɔɪ]	to move soldiers or weapons into a position where they are ready for military action
		vt. 部署；展开
		The president said he had no intention of deploying ground troops. 总统说他无意调遣地面部队。

译文

使用新的检查技术通过安检乘机

由于在六个运输安全管理局（TSA）安检点安装了七台最先进的计算机断层摄影（CT）扫描仪，迈阿密国际机场在后新冠肺炎时代的安检变得更加容易。现在允许乘客将笔记本电脑和其他电子设备放在随身行李中，通过带有 CT 扫描仪的安检通道。

新技术通过创建可在三个轴上查看和旋转的 3D 图像来提供改进的爆炸物检测筛查，以便 TSA 官员进行彻底的视觉图像分析。如果行李需要进一步检查，TSA 官员将对其进行检查，以确保其中没有危险物品。

"这些来自 TSA 的新扫描仪正在帮助我们简化和加快乘客的安检过程，在航空旅行中，顺畅地通过安检从未如此重要。我们很自豪能够成为首批通过 TSA 获得扩展 CT 技术的美国机场之一。"迈阿密国际机场董事兼首席执行官 Lester Sola 说。

与现有用于托运行李的 CT 技术一样，这些机器使用复杂的算法来检测爆炸物，包括液体爆炸物。CT 安检点设备的所需空间比行李检查设备的空间小，以便在有限的乘客安检区空间内提供停留处。

"TSA 专注于尽快在机场测试、采购和部署额外的 CT 系统，并正在继续开发增强算法以应对不断变化的航空威胁，同时减少解决因警报所需的人工检查行李次数，从而提高运营效率和实现自动检测。这七个单元加入了之前安装的另外三个单元，MIA 成为该国首批开始在 TSA 检查站推出这项技术的机场之一。"迈阿密国际机场说。

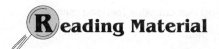

How to Survive a Plane Crash

The chances of dying on a commercial airline flight are actually as low as 9 million to 1. That said, a lot can go wrong at 33,000 feet (10,000 m) above the ground, and if you're unlucky enough to be aboard when something does, the decisions you make could mean the difference between life and death. Almost 95% of airplane crashes have no survivors, so even if the worst does happen, your odd isn't as bad as you might think. You can learn to prepare for each flight safety, stay calm during the crash itself, and survive the aftermath.

Part 1　Preparing for Flights Safely

1

Dress comfortably. You'll need to be able to stay warm if you survive a crash. Even if that is not a consideration, the more of your body is covered during impact, the less likely you are to receive serious injuries or burns. Wear long pants, a long-sleeve t-shirt, and sturdy, comfortable, lace-up shoes.

Loose or elaborate clothing poses a risk, as it can get snagged on obstacles in the close confines of a plane. If you know you're going to be flying over cold areas, dress appropriately, and consider keeping a jacket on your lap.

Cotton or wool clothing is also preferable as it is less flammable. Wool is preferable to cotton when flying over water, as wool does not lose its insulating properties to the degree cotton does when wet.

2

Wear sensible shoes. Although you may want to be comfortable or professional-looking on a flight, sandals or high heels make it hard to move quickly should there be an emergency. High heels are not allowed on the evacuation slides and you can cut your feet and toes on glass or get flammable liquids on or in your sandals if you wear them.

3

Sit in the tail of the aircraft. Passengers in the tail of the aircraft have 40% higher survival rates than those in the first few rows, in the event of a crash. Because a quick escape gives you the best chance for survival, it's best to get seats as close as possible to an exit, on the aisle, and in the back of the plane.

Yes, it's actually statistically safer to fly economy than first-class. Save money and stay safer.

4

Read the safety card and listen to the pre-flight safety speech. Yes, you may have heard it all before, and you'll probably never need it, but if you keep your headphones on during the pre-flight instructions or ignore the safety card, you'll be missing out on information that could be vital in the event of a crash.

Don't assume you know it all already, either. Every type of airplane has different safety instructions.

If you're sitting in an exit row, study the door and make sure you know how to open it if you need to. In normal circumstances the flight attendant will open the door, but if they are dead or injured, you'll need to do it.

5

Count the number of seats between your seat and the exit row. Find the exit closest to you, and count the number of seats that it'll take to get to it. If the plane crashes, it could be smoky, loud, or confusing in the cabin afterward. If you need to escape, you might have to feel your way to the exit, which will be a lot easier if you know where it is and how far.

You might even write down the number in pen on your hand, so you'll have a quick reference if you need to.

6

Keep your seat belt on at all times. Every centimeter of slack in your seat belt triples the G-Force you'll experience in the crash, so keep your seat belt properly tightened at all times you're on the aircraft.

Push the belt down as low over your pelvis as possible. You should be able to feel the upper ridge of the pelvis above the upper edge of the belt, which helps to brace you in an emergency much better than your soft stomach.

Leave your belt on, even if you're sleeping. If something happens while you're out, you'll be glad to have the restraints in place.

Part 2 Bracing on Impact

1

Assess the situation. Try to determine what surface the plane will land on so you can customize your preparations. If you're going to be landing in water, for example, you'll want to put your life vest on, though you need to wait to inflate it until you're out of the plane. If you're going to be landing in cold weather, you should try to get a blanket or jacket to keep you warm once outside.

Plot out the general course you'll be on ahead of time, so you'll have some idea of where you are when the plane crashes. If you're flying from Iowa to California, you can be fairly certain you won't be landing in the ocean.

Use the time before the crash to find your exit. If the plane is going to crash, you almost always have several minutes to prepare before impact. Use this time to once again review where the exits are.

2

Prepare your space as much as possible. If you know you're going to crash, return your seat back to its full upright position and stow away any loose items that could become hazardous, if at all possible. Zip up your jacket and make sure your shoes are tied tightly to your feet. Then assume one of two standard brace positions used for surviving a plane crash and try to remain calm.

In either position, your feet should be flat on the floor and further back than your knees to reduce injuries to your feet and legs, which you will need in order to successfully exit the craft after impact. Place your legs as far under the seat as possible to avoid breaking your shin bones.

3

Brace yourself against the seat in front of you. If the seat in front of you is close enough to reach, place one hand palm-down on the back of that seat, then cross the other hand palm-down over the first hand. Rest your forehead against your hands. Keep your fingers unlaced.

It's also sometimes recommended that you put your head directly against the seat in front of you and lace your fingers behind your head, tucking your upper arms against the sides of your head to cradle it.

Bend forward, if there's no seat in front of you. If you don't have a seat close in front of you, bend forward and put your chest on your thighs and your head between your knees. Cross your wrists in front of your lower calves, and grab your ankles.

4

Try and remain calm. It can be easy to get swept up in the pandemonium immediately preceding and following a crash. Keep a cool head, though, and you're more likely to get out alive. Remember that even in the worst wrecks, you do have a chance of survival. You'll need to be able to think methodically and rationally to maximize that chance.

5

Put on your life jacket but do not inflate it, in the case of a crash in water. If you inflate it in the plane, when it starts to fill up with water, the life jacket will force you upwards against the cabin roof and it will be very hard to swim back down, leaving you trapped. Instead, hold your breath and swim out, once you're out, inflate it.

6

Put your oxygen mask on before assisting others. You've probably heard this on every commercial flight you've been on, but it's worth repeating. If the integrity of the cabin is compromised, you have only about 15 seconds or less to start breathing through your oxygen mask before you are rendered unconscious.

While you may feel an impulse to first help your children or the elderly passenger sitting next to you, you'll be no good to anyone if you don't remain conscious. Also, remember that you can put somebody else's oxygen mask on even if they're unconscious. This might help save their life.

Part 3　Surviving the Crash

1

Protect yourself from smoke. Fire and smoke are responsible for the largest percentage of crash fatalities. The smoke in an airplane fire can be very thick and highly toxic, so cover your nose and mouth with a cloth to avoid breathing it in. If possible, moisten the cloth to provide extra protection.

Stay low as you escape, to duck under the level of smoke. It might not seem like a big deal, but passing out due to smoke inhalation is one of the most dangerous things that can happen during this critical period.

2

Get out of the airplane as quickly as possible. According to the National Transportation Safety Board (NTSB), 68 percent of plane crash deaths are due to post-crash fire, not injuries sustained in the crash itself. It's critical to get out of the aircraft without delay. If fire or smoke is present, you will generally have less than two minutes to safely exit the plane.

Make sure the exit you choose is safe. Look through the window to determine if there is fire or some other hazard outside of an exit. If there is, try the exit across the plane, or proceed to another set of exits.

3

Listen to the flight attendants' post-crash instructions. Flight attendants undergo rigorous training to make sure they know what to do in the event of a crash. If a flight attendant is able to instruct or assist you, listen closely and cooperate to increase everyone's chances of survival.

4

Ditch your stuff. Don't try to rescue your belongings. It's common sense, but still some people don't seem to get it. Leave everything behind. Rescuing your belongings will only slow you down.

If you end up needing to salvage supplies from the plane crash site, worry about that later. Right now, you need to make sure that you get clear of the wreckage and find some safe cover.

Get out now.

5

Get at least 500 feet (152.4 m) upwind from the wreckage. If you're stranded in a remote area, the best thing to do usually is to stay close to the aircraft to await rescuers. You don't want to be too close, though. Fire or explosion can happen at any time after a crash, so put some distance between you and the plane. If the crash is in open-water, swim as far away from the plane wreckage as possible.

6

Stay in one place, but pay attention to what needs to happen. While it's essential to stay calm after a crash, you also need to recognize when you need to act and do so swiftly. Help out people who are struggling and tend to people's wounds using basic first aid available.

Attend to your own wounds if at all possible. Check yourself for cuts and other abrasions, and apply pressure if necessary. Stay in one place to reduce the chance of exacerbating internal injuries.

Negative panic is a strange inability to react assertively and appropriately to the situation. For example, a person may just remain in his or her seat instead of heading toward the exit. Watch out for this in your fellow passengers or traveling companions.

7

Call Emergency Services and wait for rescue. You stand a much higher chance of surviving if you just stay put. Don't wander off and look for help, or try to find something close by. If your plane went down, there will be people on the way quickly, and you want to be there when they arrive. Just stay put.

Tips

The one exception to the "leave everything behind" rule may be a jacket or blanket, and you should only consider carrying that if you have it ready to go at impact. While having appropriate clothing may save your life if you're stranded for a while, you first have to get out of the aircraft safely.

Place your baggage beneath the seat in front of you. It can help prevent your legs from snapping under the seat.

Don't travel by plane if you have a bad heart or breathing problem.

If you have no time to prepare for the crash and you forget some of these instructions, you can find much of the most important information in the safety card in the seat back pocket in front of you.

Stay calm. The calmer, the better.

If you can find a pillow or something similarly soft to protect your head during impact, use it.

Remove sharp objects—pens, pencils, etc.—from your pockets before a crash. Better yet, don't carry them at all. Nearly any loose object on a plane can become a deadly projectile in the event of a crash.

In the event of a water landing, remove your shoes and excess clothes before or immediately after entering the water. This will make swimming and floating easier.

It's quite common for people to forget how to unbuckle their seat belts after a crash. It seems easy enough, but in your dazed condition the first instinct is often to try to push a button as you would for a car seat belt. When that doesn't work, it's easy to panic. Before impact, make a mental note to remember how to quickly and easily unbuckle your seat belt.

Save yourself before others!

Warnings

Don't push other passengers. An orderly exit increases everybody's chance of survival, and if you panic and start shoving, you may be faced with retaliation.

When landing in water, do not inflate your life vest until you are outside of the aircraft. If you do, you run the risk of becoming trapped when the aircraft fills with water.

Avoid excessive alcohol consumption before or during a flight. Alcohol impairs your ability to quickly and methodically react to the crash and evacuate the plane.

Avoid wearing synthetic fabrics while traveling by plane. If a fire breaks out in the cabin, these materials will melt to your skin.

Never hold your infant or toddler on your lap. While it may be cheaper than buying a seat, your child is almost guaranteed not to survive if you are holding him or her. Get a seat for your child and use an approved child restraint system.

Don't get down on the floor of the plane. If there is smoke in the cabin, try to stay low, but do not crawl. You will likely be trampled or injured by other passengers attempting to escape in the low-visibility conditions.

 **E**xercises

1. Vocabulary

(1) The bomb was packed with several pounds of high ( ).

   A. burst   B. explosive   C. explode   D. blast

(2) Early ( ) of cancers is vitally important.

A. inspection   B. examination   C. detection   D. test

(3) We have developed rapid order processing to ( ) deliveries to customers.

 A. expedite   B. speed   C. accelerate   D. strengthen

(4) Despite the recession the company is confident of further ( ).

 A. enlargement   B. altitude   C. heighten   D. expansion

(5) Medical techniques are becoming more ( ) all the time.

 A. conciseness   B. simplicity   C. complex   D. sophisticated

2. Dialogue

(1) P: What kind of things can not be taken on the plane?

 O:（禁止在飞机上携带任何武器、弹药、攻击性工具和易燃、易爆、腐蚀性、放射性、有毒物品。）

 P: Thank you.

(2) P: Does everyone have to receive a personal search?

 O: Yes.（对所有的国际国内乘客都进行人身检查。）

 P: What will happen to me if I refuse the security check?

 O:（任何拒绝接受检查的乘客都会被拒绝登机。）

3. Translate

(1) One-Stop Services, One Map for Operations, and One Network for Security are all developed using the Huawei Horizon Digital Platform, with multiple new technologies integrated, such as big data, AI, ICP, and video cloud.

(2) Driven by the new concept of digital transformation, we comprehensively plan new blueprints for smart airport construction and build digital new platforms by category.

(3) It's surveillance for the security area to systems for apron and runway monitoring all the way to the optimization of business processes through video-based data acquisition.

(4) Video security solutions provide a holistic coverage of the airport indoor areas.

(5) These new scanners from the TSA are helping us streamline and expedite the screening process for our passengers.

 ialogue

Control of Access

Dialogue 1

O: Excuse me, sir. Show me your pass, please.

P: OK, here you are. Could I go through that staff entrance.

O: Sorry, I need the restricted area permit for the airport. This is only a temporary badge. You have to take out your identity card and go through that screening checkpoint.

P: Fine.

O: Thank you for your cooperation.

Dialogue 2

O: Excuse me, are you going to join the crew? Please go through the security screening checkpoint.

P: OK. Then my luggage will be exempted from inspection?

O: Sorry, sir. As a crew member, you and your carry-on baggage should go through the security screening procedures.

P: OK.

O: Thanks a lot.

Dialogue 3

O: Excuse me, sir. Your pass has expired.

P: What should I do?

O: You can apply for a new pass at the airport public security bureau.

P: OK. Thank you.

O: My pleasure.

Text

CT Scanners at Security Checkpoints

The exponential growth in air traffic demand calls for new solutions that can **guarantee** efficiency, without compromising the passenger experience.

Whether it is for business or for leisure, airport passengers seek a smooth and fluid experience at the airport. In turn, airports are eager to simplify the journey across the airport and let passengers enjoy what the airport has to offer. This has become even more important as non-aeronautical **revenue** streams, such as retail, are becoming vital for an airports' financial stability.

Looking at the steps of the average passenger journey within the airport, it is possible to identify six main touchpoints:

1. Transport to the airport;

2. Check-in and luggage drop-off;

3. **Immigration**/passport control;

4. Security checkpoints;

5. Luggage collection;

6. Transport from the airport.

Several of these have been hugely **revolutionized** by new technologies that now allow for a much smoother passenger experience. One of the most successful implementations is the self-service bag drop. Several examples of this innovative solution can be found at many airports across the world and passengers are now accustomed to this service that **considerably** shortens the waiting time to drop off luggage. This **innovation** has been the natural evolution of the already established online check-in option.

Another touchpoint that has been automated is passport controls; in fact, many airports have implemented smart border control systems. Travellers can now pass through smart gates that are equipped with RFID scanners, significantly decreasing the wait time. As a consequence, the efficiency of the screening process has been dramatically increased, with security personnel only required to **intervene** in specific situations.

However, this wave of innovation has not yet reached all areas of the airport. For instance, cabin baggage security screening operations, which are a sensible phase of the passengers' journey, still cause stress for many passengers because of the unexpected queues and unclear screening procedures.

ECAC, TSA, CATSA among other international entities worldwide are already collaborating with airports to test computed tomography (CT) scanners, as an alternative to traditional X-ray machines. This technology has been used for years for checked luggage and technical improvements now make it possible to use them for cabin baggage as well.

The implementation of CT scanners would allow for the update of the security screening "concept of operations" (CONOPS), with a strong positive impact on passengers' experience. Taking as the example ECAC's CONOPS for CT scanners (i.e., ECAC C3), laptops and liquids could possibly be left within cabin baggage. Passengers would not need to take any object out of their cabin luggage and efficiency would be increased. In fact, with the new procedure, passengers divested time would drop considerably, as well as the average number of trays used per passenger.

Harmonizing and simplifying procedures to take full advantage of technical innovations.

However great these innovations may be, the transition to new standards will require several months, if not years, and collective efforts from all industry players is needed to harmonize these processes where possible. More importantly, the simplification of certain certification processes within the value chain could significantly **enhance** the adoption of such policies sooner rather than later.

In light of this inevitable technological improvement, the aviation industry should work to translate this technical and operational improvement into a better experience for passengers with proper communication streams. The transition to CT scanners could be the last piece that transcends the passengers' journey into a unique 360 degree airport experience.

Vocabulary

checkpoint	['tʃekpɔɪnt]	a place, especially on a border between two countries, where people have to stop so their vehicles and documents can be checked n. (边防) 检查站; 边防关卡 Soldiers opened fire on a car which failed to stop at an army checkpoint. 士兵们向一辆没在军事检查站停下来的汽车开了火。
guarantee	[ˌɡærən'tiː]	to promise to do sth; to promise sth will happen vt. 保证; 担保 A famous old name on a firm is not necessarily a guarantee of quality. 公司的老字号并不一定能保证质量。
revenue	['revənjuː]	the money that a government receives from taxes or that an organization, etc. receives from its business n. 税收收入; 财政收入; 收益 The company's annual revenues rose by 30%. 公司的年收入增加了30%。
immigration	[ˌɪmɪ'ɡreɪʃn]	the process of coming to live permanently in a country that is not your own; the number of people who do this n. 移居 (入境); 移民人数, 外来移民; 移居 laws restricting immigration into the US 美国限制外来移民的法律
revolutionize	[ˌrevə'luːʃənaɪz]	to completely change the way that sth is done v. 彻底改变; 完全变革, 发动革命, 推翻原有政府; 从事革命; 彻底改革, 彻底改变; 灌输革命信念 Aerial photography has revolutionized the study of archaeology. 航空摄影已经给考古学研究带来了一场革命。
considerably	[kən'sɪdərəbli]	much; a lot

adv. 相当地；非常地，非常；很；相当多地

He has gone down considerably in my estimation. 我对他的评价已经大大降低了

innovation	[ˌɪnə'veɪʃn]	the introduction of new things, ideas or ways of doing sth. *n.*（新事物、思想或方法的）创造；创新；改革新方法 We must promote originality, inspire creativity and encourage innovation. 我们必须提倡独创性，激发创造力，鼓励创新。
intervene	[ˌɪntə'viːn]	If you intervene in a situation, you become involved in it and try to change it. *v.* 出面；介入；阻碍；干扰；插嘴；介于……之间； The Government is doing nothing to intervene in the crisis. 政府没有采取任何行动对这次危机进行干预。
harmonize	['hɑːmənaɪz]	If two or more things harmonize with each other, they fit in well with each other. *vt.* 彼此协调，使和谐；使一致； *vi.* 协调；和谐； The new building does not harmonize with its surroundings. 那栋新楼与周围环境不协调。
enhance	[ɪn'hɑːns]	to increase or further improve the good quality, value or status of sb./sth. *vt.* 提高；加强；增加 This is an opportunity to enhance the reputation of the company. 这是提高公司声誉的机会。

译文

安全检查站的 **CT** 扫描仪

空中交通需求的迅猛增长要求新的解决方案，既能保证效率，又不影响乘客体验。

无论是商务出行还是休闲出行，机场乘客都希望获得顺畅的体验。反过来，机场也渴望简化机场的流程，让乘客享受机场所提供的一切。随着零售业等非航空收入流对机场的财务稳定变得至关重要，这一点变得更加重要。

查看机场内乘客平均旅程的步骤，可以确定六个主要节点：

（1）前往机场；

（2）办理登机手续和行李寄存；

（3）入境/护照检查；

（4）安全检查站；

（5）行李提取；

（6）机场交通。

其中一些节点已经被新技术彻底改变，现在可以为乘客提供更顺畅的体验。最成功的实践之一是自助行李托运。在世界各地的许多机场，都可以找到几个这种创新解决方案的例子，乘客现在已经习惯了这项服务，它大大缩短了托运行李的等待时间。这项创新已经成为之前建立的在线值机的自然演化结果。

另一个自动化的节点是护照检查；事实上，许多机场已经实施了智能边境管制系统。旅客现在可以通过配备 RFID 扫描仪的智能安检门，大大减少了等待时间。因此，安检过程的效率显著提高，安检人员只需要在特定情况下进行人工检查。

然而，这波创新浪潮尚未波及机场的所有领域。例如，随身行李安检操作是乘客旅行中的一个合理阶段，由于意外排队和不清楚检查程序，仍然给许多乘客带来压力。

ECAC、TSA、CATSA 等全球其他国际实体已经与机场合作测试计算机断层摄影（CT）扫描仪，作为传统 X 光机的替代品。这项技术已用于托运行李检查很多年了，现在技术改进，使其检查随身行李成为可能。

CT 扫描仪的实施将允许更新安全检查"操作概念"（CONOPS），对乘客体验产生了强烈的积极影响。以 ECAC 的 CT 扫描仪 CONOPS（ECAC C3）为例，笔记本电脑和液体可能会留在随身行李中。乘客无须从随身行李中取出任何物品，从而提高效率。事实上，采用新程序后，乘客的过检时间将大大减少，每位旅客使用放置随身物品托盘的平均数量也减少了。

协调和简化程序以充分利用技术创新。

无论这些创新多么伟大，向新标准的过渡都需要几个月甚至几年的时间，并且需要所有行业参与者的共同努力，以尽可能协调这些流程。更重要的是，价值链中某些认证流程的简化，可以尽早地显著促进此类政策的采用。

鉴于这种不可避免的技术进步，民航业应致力于将这种技术和运营改进转化为有良好交通流的更好的旅客体验。向 CT 扫描仪的过渡，可能是最后一个超越乘客旅行的，进入独特的机场 360° 全方位体验的环节。

Reading Material

How to Practice Airplane Etiquette

When traveling by air, you're sometimes forced to rub elbows (literally) with people you don't know. In close quarters and for extended periods of time, a little consideration can go a long way. To make a flight as smooth as possible for both yourself and others (and to avoid dirty looks) practice airplane etiquette as follows.

Part 1   Storing Your Belongings

1

Carry your bag in front of you and low to the ground as you walk down the aisle in search of your seat. Holding it up and at your sides will inevitably knock seated passengers on their arms, shoulders, and heads. You can pull it along if it has wheels.

2

Utilize the overhead space above your own seat row. Do not place your bags in the overhead at the front of the plane unless you are sitting in that row. Don't put your bag in a bin near the front of the plane for a quick exit — it means someone else will have to wait until the entire plane has emptied to walk back to get their bag. Taking the storage space of other passengers is rude and can potentially delay departure as they search for storage.

3

Avoid hogging the aisle. Remember that space is limited on board. Always be swift and alert while putting things in the overhead lockers, as other people need the aisle space to get around you and to their seat. Place the items that you will frequently use in your seat back pocket or under the seat in front of you.

4

Take care when retrieving luggage from the overhead compartment! It may be positioned to fall on you or someone else. If you have a lot of bulky, heavy luggage in the overhead bin, wait until others have left before standing and blocking other people from leaving the plane (they may have another flight to get to), or ask somebody to help you get your luggage down while everybody is waiting to leave the plane. This will help with traffic flow and allows all passengers to leave the plane as fast as possible.

Part 2　Sitting with Respect

1

Keep your chair upright at least until you're told it can be reclined. Don't lean your chair back as soon as you get on. When you do recline your chair, do it slowly. Otherwise, you risk bumping the head of the unsuspecting passenger behind you who's getting something from the bag at her feet, or you could knock over the drink on his or her tray. Remember to return the seat back to the upright position during meal and drink servings, or if possible, wait until food and beverages are finished being served and cleaned up.

2

Check behind you — is that person tall, or does he/she have a child on his/her lap? If so, consider keeping your seat upright out of consideration, especially if it's a short flight. By reclining, you're taking space away from the passenger behind you; you may be more comfortable, but at someone else's expense. You can also ask them if reclining your seat would be all right. If you're someone who can't make yourself comfortable without reclining, then do your best to choose an aisle, bulkhead, or exit row seat when booking the flight so the person behind you has extra space.

3

If you're a tall/big person or have a child on your lap and know that having the seat in front of you reclined will make you uncomfortable, choose a bulkhead or exit row seat (unless you have a child, in which case you should never choose an exit row seat). Not only will you have more space, but the person in front of you will also have more space and may decide not to recline their seat out of consideration for you. If you sit in the middle, however, the person in front of you is cramped, as well, and will probably want to recline their seat, whether you like it or not.

4

If you are traveling with one or more children, keep a close eye on them. Children have a tendency to bump, kick, or yank the seat in front of them without realizing it throughout the flight, which can make the person in front of them very uncomfortable. It's difficult enough to control some children on a long flight, but it's even more difficult to deal with an angry passenger in front of you.

If your children has difficulty flying, do everything you can to relax the children so you do not disturb other passengers nearby. Bring plenty of books, games, snacks and other things to keep your children quietly occupied.

You can also try walking to the galley area of the plane to stretch your children's legs.

Change diapers in the restroom on the plane. In most restrooms there are changing tables and trash bins for diaper disposal.

When breastfeeding, use a drape, both for your own privacy and for the comfort of other passengers.

5

If another passenger breaches etiquette by, for example, constantly thumping or yanking your seat back, and refuses your polite request not to do so, don't get any further involved. Ask a flight attendant to handle the situation, and if they can't or even won't (this does happen), ask politely but insistently for the chief flight attendant (purser) to handle it.

6

Avoid grabbing the back of the seat in front of you. Grabbing the seat back as you walk in the aisle or in your row can be unpleasantly jarring to the person sitting in it. Copy the flight attendants who balance themselves in the aisle by grabbing the luggage compartments above their heads, rather than the seat backs.

Part 3　Respecting Personal Space

1

No matter how much you love to make new friends on the plane, the person next to you might rather get some work done, or simply may not feel like being chatty. If a friendly comment gets a minimal answer, take the hint and leave them be. If you're traveling with children, try to avoid letting them think of passengers as playmates. Some passengers will smile to be polite, but may not be interested in playing "peek a boo" with the children.

2

If you want to watch a movie on your personal DVD player, keep in mind your screen is visible to those behind you. If your movie has nudity, graphic violence, etc. it may offend the more sensitive viewers (e.g. children) looking on. Using a smaller, handheld device to view movies, such as on an iPod Touch, may be more practical in this situation.

3

Watch your elbows. If you're reading a newspaper or using a laptop, try not to let your elbows "spill over" onto someone else's personal space. Do your best not to hog the arm rests, especially if the person next to you is in the middle and has limited space to begin with.

Make use of your own arm rest and headphone plug outlet. Don't use someone else's because it's more convenient for you.

4

Keep your stuff close. If you put a bag or a jacket at your feet, don't let it spill over onto the legs or feet of the person sitting next to you.

5

Get your own reading material — don't read theirs. They'll notice, and it's nosy and rude.

If you're stuck in an aisle seat but still want to enjoy the view, don't lean over the person next to you to look out the window.

6

Pack headphones for any portable electronics, especially games and DVD players. Hearing someone else's music and sounds can be very irritating.

7

Don't get drunk during (or before) the flight. You may be having the time of your life, but your fellow passengers may not think so (there are airlines which don't allow any passengers on board suspected of being over the limit on alcohol consumption).

Part 4　Moving with Care

1

Be considerate of other passengers when you exit the plane. Resist the urge to push your way out first; let those nearest the exit disembark the plane first. When your turn comes, move quickly so people with connecting flights can make it in time.

2

If you know you'll need a connecting flight, think ahead and book your flight early so you can get a seat up front and exit quickly.

3

Get up to use the lavatory or to walk around only when necessary. Go through your carry-on luggage at intervals. If you need something, think ahead and retrieve items you might need later on during the flight.

4

When you get up, don't yank on the seat in front of you for support; use the seat armrests. If you want to get up but there is one or more passengers between you and the aisle, politely request that they get up to let you pass. Don't try to clamber over them; apart from the discomfort this will inevitably cause, you might injure yourself/them if you lose your balance and fall.

Tips

Clean up after yourself. Don't leave your trash stuffed in the seat pocket, blankets and pillows thrown about, crackers littered all over the seat and floor, etc. An airplane seat should be left as close as possible to how it was found. This will make "flipping the airplane" much faster for the maintenance crew and keep flights on time.

If you plan on taking a sleeping pill, opt for a window seat so passengers aren't required to climb over you in order to access the restroom.

At security, the fewer "things" you are carrying, the better. Leave all your jewelry, keys, spare change, iPod, phone, newspaper etc, in your bag. If you think your belt might set off the metal detector, take it off before security, put it in your bag, so you can put it back on afterward.

Remember that babies and children don't understand airplanes and pressure differences in their ears. Even the best behaved baby will cry during the takeoff and descent portion of the flight. Feeding a baby or giving him a pacifier can help; the sucking motion can help equalize pressure.

When movies start, ask the passenger next to you if they'd prefer to have the window shade down. The sun's rays can create an annoying glare on the television monitor, making it harder to see a view from a specific seat in the airplane. The person next to you may or may not be bothered by this; sometimes they'd prefer to have the light from the window.

Make sure you are aware of the new security rules (amount of allowable liquids in a small plastic ziplock bag etc). Security checks are delayed every time somebody tries to get through with items which are not allowed.

Keep your conversations to a low whisper if you're traveling with someone. If you speak too loudly, you'll interrupt someone's sleep or annoy your fellow passengers.

If you have a habit of removing your shoes because you're flying a long distance, make sure you don't have foot odor.

At the baggage claim, stand back from the carousel until you see your bag approaching, then step forward to retrieve it.

Do not put your feet up on the bulkhead if you are sitting by it. It's ill-mannered. If you must raise your feet, put your bag on the floor and put your feet on that.

Warnings

Remember that even if you wear headphones while you listen to loud music, your direct neighbor can hear it, and will likely be less than pleased about it. Turn your music player to a more moderate level for the flight.

Do not pack strong smelling foods (e.g. tuna sandwiches, anything with onions, deli, etc.) to eat on the plane. Your fellow passengers may be sensitive to the smell.

Exercises

1. Vocabulary

(1) Soldiers opened fire on a car which failed to stop at an army (   ).

    A. monitoring   B. surveillance   C. checkpoint   D. examination

(2) A famous old name on a firm is not necessarily a (   ) of quality.

    A. insurance   B. safe   C. ensure   D. guarantee

(3) The company's annual (   ) rose by 30%.

    A. distribution   B. revenues   C. glory   D. harvest

(4) The Government is doing nothing to (   ) in the crisis.

    A. intervene   B. supervise   C. interfere   D. disturb

(5) This is an opportunity to (   ) the reputation of the company.

    A. increase   B. enhance   C. promote   D. broaden

2. Dialogue

(1) O: Excuse me, （您是加入机组吗?） Please go through the security screening checkpoint.

    P: OK. Then is my luggage exempted from inspection?

    O: Sorry, sir. As a crew member, （您本人和您的行李都需要安全检查。）

(2) O: Excuse me, sir. （您的通行证过期了。）

    P: What should I do?

    O: （您可以去公安局申请新通行证。）

    P: OK. Thank you.

    O: My pleasure.

3. Translate

（1）借助适用于航站楼外部区域的视频技术解决方案，例如自动车牌识别（ANPR），机场运营商可确保安全和提升旅客体验。

（2）视频分析技术（例如自动人数统计）可用于更有效地管理访客流量。通过这种方式，机场运营商可以优化等待时间，例如在值机、安检或身份检查时。

（3）Dallmeier ROMS（跑道光学监控解决方案）使机场运营商只需要几个摄像系统和安装点，即可监控数公里的跑道。

（4）以最少数量的摄像机覆盖较大的面积，可以在数字塔中高效地工作。

（5）美国运输安全管理局表示，虽然目前还没有涉及爆炸粉末的具体威胁，但新装备将有助于防止恐怖分子登上飞机，并将粉末作为简易爆炸装置的部件。

Lesson One

1. Vocabulary

（1）D　　（2）D　　（3）B　　（4）A　　（5）D

2. Dialogue

（1）O: Yes, May I have your passport and boarding pass, please?

　　P: Here you are.

（2）O: Sorry, it seems there is something wrong with passport. Please wait here for a moment.

3. Translate

（1）现在只需要十多分钟即可完成从机场入口到登机口所有必要的登机程序。

（2）就在上周，我们还被要求在登机前扫描电子登机牌或身份证，但现在我们可以直接借助面部识别（FR）技术登机。

（3）通过移动应用程序/在线/自助服务亭办理登机手续，收到登机牌后，您可以使用该登机牌办理行李托运。

（4）验证完成后，您可以在屏幕上查看您的航班详情。

（5）飞机，比空气重的固定翼飞机，由螺旋桨或高速喷气机推进，由空气对其机翼的动态反应提供支持。

Lesson Two

1. Vocabulary

（1）B　　（2）B　　（3）C　　（4）A　　（5）D

2. Dialogue

（1）O: Excuse me, sir. Please put all your bags on the belt to be checked.

　　P: OK.

　　O: Take off your shoes, take the personal items out of your pockets, and place it all into the trays, please.

（2）O: Oh, things like keys, coins, cell phone, cigarettes, wallet, and so on.

　　P: And should I take off my watch as well?

　　O: Yes, of course.

3. Translate

（1）飞机的基本组成是机身、飞行维持机翼系统、稳定尾翼、高度控制装置（如方向舵）、推力提供动力源和着陆支持系统。

（2）大多数飞机设计为在陆地上起降；水上飞机适合在水面上着陆，舰载飞机被改装用于高速短距离起降。

（3）随着阿联酋与世界多个国家之间的免检疫旅行走廊的开通，迪拜的航空业一直处于恢复重要国际航空服务的全球运动的前沿。

（4）我们在机场安全、运营和服务方面已经初步取得了新的进展。

（5）通过积极运用大数据、人工智能等新技术，创新了智慧机场的建设模式。

Lesson Three

1. Vocabulary

（1）D　　（2）B　　（3）A　　（4）C　　（5）A

2. Dialogue

（1）O: Excuse me, do you still have any metal items on you?

　　P: No. My pockets are empty.

（2）O: Please take off your shoes and step over here. Stand on the platform, please. Your shoes should be x-rayed separately.

　　P: But, is the floor clean?

　　O: Don't worry. The mat has been disinfected. Now hold out your arms and stand with your feet apart please.

3. Translate

（1）You may bring liquids, aerosols, and gels in your cabin luggage as long as they do not exceed a maximum volume of 100ml for each item, carried in one resealable, transparent plastic bag no more than 1-litre in capacity per passenger.

（2）There are security restrictions in the United States and Australia/New Zealand on the carriage of certain types of powders into the cabin of an aircraft, limiting maximum volume to 350 ml (12 oz).

（3）You may bring any volume of liquid, aerosol and gel items purchased at Duty Free stores in your hand luggage, provided you keep your proof of purchase and kept in a sealed, tamper-evident bag.

（4）Medicines and toiletries in limited quantities and alcoholic beverages may be carried in checked or cabin baggage (maximum 2 litres or 2 kg).

（5）Alliance Airlines reserves the right to determine what items are unsuitable for carriage because they are dangerous, unsafe or because of their weight, size, shape or character, or which are fragile or perishable.

Lesson Four

1. Vocabulary

（1）B　　（2）A　　（3）D　　（4）B　　（5）A

2. Dialogue

（1）O: I need you to open your bag and check the contents.

　　P: Of course you can check my bag.

（2）O: Is this your bag? I must open it for a further check.

　　O: What is inside these small bottles?

　　P: They are bottles of makeup.

3. Translate

（1）危险品是可能危及飞机、乘客或货物安全的物品。

（2）美国运输安全管理局给机场检查站官员一种新工具：测试爆炸粉末的工具包。

（3）如果 X 光机检测到潜在的危险粉末，则将样品与溶液混合进行测试。

（4）旅客仍然可以携带婴儿配方奶粉、化妆品和药品等粉末登上飞机。

（5）大多数乘客不会注意到检查点程序有任何不同，这只是又一层安全检查，有助于增强我们的爆炸检测能力。

Lesson Five

1. Vocabulary

（2）C　　（2）A　　（3）B　　（4）A　　（5）A

2. Dialogue

（1）P:　My flight will depart Gate 25. Would you please tell me how to get there?

　　O:　Please go straight and turn left in 100 meters. Gate 25 is at the end of the corridor.

（2）P:　How can I find the Gate?

　　O:　It will be easy to find. Each gate is clearly marked.

3. Translate

（1）从 2018 年 6 月 30 日起，如果您从国际出发点前往美国，携带行李中有大于 350 ml 或 12 盎司的粉状物质，可能需要在中央检查点进行额外的检查。

（2）随身携带的超过 12 盎司或 350 ml 在中央检查站无法处理的粉状物质，将不被允许进入机舱，并将被处置。

（3）为方便起见，将粉末放在托运行李里。

（4）这些措施已经在美国全国各地的机场实施，以识别和防止潜在的危险物品被带上飞机。

（5）美国机场检查站允许的随身行李没有改变。

Lesson Six

1. Vocabulary

（1）A　　（2）B　　（3）C　　（4）B　　（5）D

2. Dialogue

（1）O:　Excuse me, whose bag is this?

　　P:　Oh, it's mine. Is there anything wrong?

（2）O:　Yes, something in the baggage is leaking.

　　P:　Oh, I can smell it. It's perfume. I dropped my bag on the ground when I got out of the taxi. It must have broken.

3. Translate

（1）Passengers will still pass their carry-on bags through an X ray machine.

（2）If the X-ray machine detects a potentially hazardous powder, the powder container will be removed, a small sample will be taken and mixed with a solution for testing.

（3）During pilot tests late last year, a "very small percentage" of the baggage stream required additional tests.

（4）The vast majority of common powders — infant formula, medication and makeup — did not need additional screening.

（5）If powder does need another level of screening, it will be done in a way that avoids contamination of the product, and passengers will be made aware of the test result.

Lesson Seven

1. Vocabulary

（1）A　　（2）A　　（3）B　　（4）D　　（5）A

2. Dialogue

（1）P:　Excuse me, I lost my bag.

　　O:　Please describe your bag, such as the size, color, and so on.

　　P:　It is a blue carry-on bag and it has a red tag on it.

（2）P:　I'm here to meet my friend. The flight number is CA174. Has the flight arrived to the airport?

　　O:　I'm not sure. You can check an electronic display screen.

3. Translate

（1）任何被确定为潜在威胁的粉末都将不允许进入安全区域。

（2）过去，运输安全官员必须依靠运输安全管理局的爆炸物专家或当地执法部门来检查需要额外筛查的粉末。

（3）运输安全管理局表示，这些装备每套售价为 145 美元。

（4）三年前，在英国当局发现一起使用易燃液体摧毁至少 7 架跨大西洋客机的阴谋后，运输安全管理局及其海外同行，对乘客可能携带的液体数量实施了严格限制。

（5）这些限制仍然存在。

Lesson Eight

1. Vocabulary

（1）B　　（2）C　　（3）D　　（4）C　　（5）C

2. Dialogue

（1）O:　Are you a pilot?

P: Yes, I am.

O: Which airline are you working for?

P: Air China.

（2）P: I must go back to the airplane, I left my bag in the cabin.

O: Well, please wait for a few minutes, when all passengers have disembarked, you may return.

3. Translate

（1）2019 年，机场推出了基于 FR 的安检、智能安检通道、简易安检平台，实现全流程自助安检，进一步提升旅客体验。

（2）安全是民航的生命线，也是深圳机场建设智能机场的重点。

（3）深圳机场利用智能机场安全运营中心（SOC）建立了全面的安全支持系统，提供从地面到空中的安全保护，形成了技术密集型、主动化的系统。

（4）该系统能够准确识别潜在风险，高效处理异常情况，全局掌控机场安全状态。

（5）它智能地将被动式机场安全管理升级为主动、准确的安全风险识别和防控。

Lesson Nine

1. Vocabulary

（1）B　　（2）C　　（3）A　　（4）D　　（5）D

2. Dialogue

（1）P: What kind of things can not be taken on the plane?

O: It's forbidden to carry any kind of weapons, ammunitions, aggressive tools and inflammable, explosive, corrosive, radioactive, poisonous articles on the plane.

P: Thank you.

（2）P: Does everyone have to receive a personal search?

O: Yes. The personal search is made on all passengers both domestic and international.

P: What will happen to me if I refuse the security check?

O: Anyone who refuses that will not be allowed to board the flight.

3. Translate

（1）一站式服务、一个运营规划图和一个安全网络，都是用华为地平线数字平台开发的，使用了多种集成新技术，如大数据、人工智能、ICP 和视频云。

（2）在数字化转型新理念的推动下，我们要全面规划智慧机场建设新蓝图，分类打造数字化新平台。

（3）通过基于视频的数据采集优化业务流程，它的监控系统对安全区域、停机坪和进出跑道的所有路径的控制系统发挥作用。

（4）视频安全解决方案可全面覆盖机场室内区域。

（5）这些来自 TSA 的新扫描仪正在帮助我们简化和加快乘客的安检过程。

Lesson Ten

1. Vocabulary

（1）C　　（2）D　　（3）B　　（4）A　　（5）B

2. Dialogue

（1）Q: Excuse me, are you going to join the crew? Please go through the security screening checkpoint.

P: OK. Then is my luggage exempted from inspection?

Q: Sorry, sir. As a crew member, you and your carry-on baggage should go through the security screening procedures

（2）O: Excuse me, sir. Your pass has expired.

P: What should I do?

O: You can apply for a new pass at the airport public security bureau.

P: OK. Thank you.

O: My pleasure.

3. Translate

（1）With video technology solutions for the outside area of the terminal, such as automatic license plate recognition (ANPR), airport operators ensure a secure and improved customer experience.

（2）Video analysis techniques (e.g. automatic people counting) can be used to manage visitor flows more efficiently. In this way, airport operators optimise waiting times, e.g. at check-in, in the security area or at ID checks.

（3）The Dallmeier ROMS (Runway Optical Monitoring Solution) enables airport operators to monitor several kilometres of runways with only a few camera systems and installation points.

（4）Covering large areas with a minimum number of cameras allows an efficient work in the Digital Tower.

（5）While there is no specific threat at this time involving explosive powders, the new kits will help protect against the possibility that terrorists could board a plane and use the powder as a component in an improvised explosive device, the TSA said.

References

[1] https://universalenroll.dhs.gov.

[2] https://www.tsa.gov/travel/frequently-asked-questions/what-are-cbp-passid-and-kno wn-traveler-number.

[3] https://www.tsa.gov/precheck/faq.

[4] https://ttp.cbp.dhs.gov.

[5] Amy Tan. Travel Planner & Founder, Planet Hoppers. Expert Interview. 12 March 2020.

[6] https://universalenroll.dhs.gov/programs/precheck.

[7] https://www.youtube.com/watch?v=RNinfd8NJHI&t=89s.

[8] https://wonderfulengineering.com/these-are-the-major-design-differences-between-a irbus-and-boeing-aircrafts.

[9] http://www.differencebetween.info/difference-between-airbus-and-boeing.

[10] https://www.youtube.com/watch?v=UEMfh-0kRJo&t=479s.

[11] https://www.self.com/story/plane-crash-survival-tips.

[12] https://lifehacker.com/how-to-survive-a-plane-crash-1820981125.

[13] http://www.cnn.com/2015/02/06/travel/plane-crash-survival-tips-feat.

[14] https://www.scientificamerican.com/article/how-to-survive-a-plane-crash.

[15] https://www.travelandleisure.com/airlines-airports/how-to-survive-a-plane-going-do wn-according-to-a-pilot.

[16] https://www.theflightexpert.com/how-to-survive-a-plane-crash.

[17] 严琴，李红伟，张莉. 民航安检英语教程[M]. 北京：中国民航出版社，2006.

[18] 张宙，刘珏，季玲玲. 民航安检英语[M]. 北京：中国民航出版社，2017.